YOUR FIRST GREAT DANE

Your First Great Dane

by

Angela Mitchell

Illustrations by Steve Tyler

PARAPRESS LTD
TUNBRIDGE WELLS

Also published by Parapress:

Musicians' Injuries: a Guide to their Understanding and Prevention
by Nicola Culf
England's One Test Wonders by Roderick Easdale

© Angela Mitchell 2000
ISBN: 1-898594-67-8
Reprinted 2009 and 2011

First published in the UK by
PARAPRESS LTD
5 Bentham Hill House
Stockland Green Road
Tunbridge Wells
Kent
TN3 0TJ

A catalogue record for this book is available
from the British Library.

Typeset in Bookman by
Vitaset, Paddock Wood, Kent

Printed and bound by The Berforts Group www.berforts.com

CONTENTS

Acknowledgement   1

Introduction   3

Finding Your Puppy (How we caught the bug)   5

Preparing for Your Puppy (Watch out, purse)   13

Bringing Your Puppy Home (Preparing for the blitz)   20

Feeding (Stoking the furnace)   27

Exercising (Get the saddle ready)   34

Playing Games (Being a spoilsport)   43

Sleeping (A quart into a pint pot)   49

Changing Shapes (From 0-30 in nine months)   54

Your Dog on his Own (Batten down the hatches)   59

The Nose to Tail Tour (Which end to avoid)   65

Dane-ish Habits (Entertaining the troops)   70

General Care (Smartening up his act)   77

Helping the Aged (one and over)   82

Final Words (Nothing like a Dane)   86

Address of National Great Dane Rescue   89

ILLUSTRATIONS

Colour plates between pages 26 and 27

1. Early days

2. & 3. A quart into a pint pot

4. & 5. A Great Dane doesn't just fit discreetly into your house

6. Hovis shows off his paces

7. But watch out for the fly-by!

8. The dignified Dane profile

9. He will always be there for you

Acknowledgement:

this book is dedicated to him,
HOVIS
for showing me how.

INTRODUCTION

I am not a vet. I am not a dog breeder or show judge. I am just an ordinary person who happened to want to own a Great Dane. Everything I have learned, I learned on the way. I have made a few mistakes. So what? That's what life is all about. My dog hasn't suffered as a result of my mistakes. He may have wondered what I was doing half the time, but he didn't complain. Much.

Some dog breeders, on reading this book, will probably tut-tut and shake their heads as, believe it or not, there are 'doggy' people out there who think us mere mortals incapable of giving a Great Dane a decent home. There are even breeders who will refuse to sell you one of their beloved puppies if you don't intend to show it. I think I can identify the reasoning behind this, but I still find it ridiculous. Surely a good home is paramount for one of their puppies, regardless of whether you wish to show it or not?

Having said that, I am not prepared to criticise the showing fraternity, as I have only a very limited knowledge of it, all of which has been witnessed purely from a spectator's point of view. Suffice it to say that it is not for me. I have my own opinion of my dog; I don't need other people telling me theirs. And, apart from that, only I am allowed to call my dog ugly. I get deeply offended if anyone else should dare.

This book has no 'Health and Diseases' chapter, as I am not qualified to instruct people on how and when to give their dogs medical treatment. The only thing I will say on the subject is: get yourself a good vet, and get to know him well. And while you're at it, give him your chequebook and a pen and tell him to help himself.

This book, therefore, has been written from my experience not only of that handful of Great Danes I know well, but also from talking to vets, talking to people 'in' Danes, as well as talking to the plain old Dane-owning Joe Public, in which I include myself. But by far the most valuable information of all has come from Hovis, and my family's experience of sharing our lives with him.

Throughout this book, I have referred to both genders as he, him and dog, as it makes for more fluent reading than having to keep reading 'he or she', 'dog or bitch'.

I hope you enjoy reading this book as much as I enjoyed writing it. It truly was a labour of love.

Angela Mitchell, 2000

FINDING YOUR PUPPY
(How we caught the bug)

I always said that when we were rich and lived in a big house we'd have a Great Dane. Well, it took thirty-three years to realise that I was never going to be rich, and therefore would only ever be a member of the three-bedroomed semi brigade, but I still yearned for a Great Dane. After a discussion with my husband and son, we decided to venture, like lambs to the slaughter, into the world of Great Dane ownership.

First, a trip to the library to rummage along its shelves. There, tucked away, was a dusty, solitary book on the breed. I believe it was *The Great Dane* by Jean Lanning, a name you will become familiar with during your Dane-owning life. Reading it from cover to cover prompted the belief that I was ready to give one of these dogs a home. Perhaps what I should have done was close the book and run, but I was on a roll. A quick telephone call to the vet to enquire about the medical history and needs of the Great Dane resulted in him informing us that, thankfully, they were still a remarkably hardy breed.

We'd already decided on a male dog because, to us, there's something about a male animal, a certain presence. If you're buying a pet, the gender of your dog is entirely down to your own personal preference. One person will say that bitches are more loyal, another will swear that dogs are. Some people claim that bitches are devious and conniving, others say they are gentle and trustworthy. The same inconsistencies are shown towards dogs; some people say that dogs have a more steady, 'laid back' temperament, yet others say they are headstrong and unreliable. Each sex has its pros and cons and only you can decide which one will be best suited to your own personality and lifestyle. On the issue of colour, we'd decided very early on that we wanted a fawn, because back then, in our opinion, fawn was what a 'proper' Great Dane should be. Now, though, having spent time around Great Danes, we have decided that our next dog is to be a harlequin, a colour we'd previously disliked. Colour again is entirely a matter of your own personal choice, although many breeders claim that of the five recognised Great Dane colours (and two unrecognised ones, the Boston and the merle), the harlequin tends to be the most intelligent dog. Once I would have dismissed this as nonsense, believing that surely colour is just that – the colour of an animal's fur. But having owned many cats of many different colours in the past, I have seen evidence to support the claim that there seems to be more to it than that. In my experience, black cats are the most intelligent, tabby cats the least.

The next step was, where to find our Great Dane? Not being 'doggy' people, we didn't even know where to begin. How about the *Yellow Pages*, we thought? Yes, there really are Great Danes in there. Have a look in yours. After what seemed like several hours of ringing round and being told either, "Yes, we have plenty of blue, black or brindle, which colour did you want?" or "Yes, we have puppies, they'll be ready in six weeks," we realised that it was going to be harder than we had first thought. I know it's wrong but, as it was our first, I was too excited to wait six weeks for our new family member. I have since learned a bit more patience and, with our next dog, I will be prepared to wait until I find the exact puppy I'm looking for, even if it has not been born, and even if it involves travelling some distance. (I don't mean to imply that Hovis was the 'wrong' dog, but, with hindsight, we should not have lined that particular breeder's large, greedy pockets with our cash.)

It may seem as if you'll never get there, but once you've met someone 'in Danes', you will then find access to many reputable Dane breeders (and some not so reputable), and possibly your new puppy. Take heart that your subsequent Danes will be much, much easier to find than your first.

We eventually found a breeder with male, fawn puppies not too far from us and arranged a visit. On our arrival, we were shown the way through some disused stables to what was hopefully going to be our dream puppy. Inside an old tack-room there was a pen where the mother, looking incredibly tired, lay suckling her pups. She stood up and walked over to greet us dragging a belly load of puppies in her wake, each one dropping off with an audible popping sound at various stages of her journey, so that by the time she reached us there was nothing left but her huge empty teats. These were so pendulous, she looked as though someone had stuck a couple of rows of semi-inflated rubber gloves to her undercarriage. She was a lovely friendly bitch, but with a desperate look about her, almost as if she were pleading with us to take every one of her puppies away with us right there and then, and just let her get one decent night of uninterrupted sleep.

While on the subject of the puppies' mother, let me say that it is absolutely vital that you see her. Apart from her presence reassuring you that you are at a breeder's, and not a 'puppy farm', her temperament is very important. While on a different occasion to see some puppies, one particular breeder showed us the mother separately with strict instructions not to go anywhere near her as she'd "have our arm off". When we questioned about the apparent over-protectiveness of the mum toward her puppies, we were told, "She's not being protective to the pups, she's just a bit nasty." Needless to say, we said our goodbyes and politely left, puppyless.

On seeing the mother, you will also get a rough idea of what your puppy is going to look like, i.e. shape of head, ear size, droop of the lips (or 'flaps', as we like to call them). It's not at all unusual for the father of the puppies not to be on site, as many breeders either don't keep a stud dog or, even if they do, they may just be introducing some 'outside blood' to their stock. And, although a lot of people will tell you to get a 'home-reared' puppy, you will find that quite a lot of Great Dane breeders don't actually keep their dogs in their houses. This is simply because of their size. Just one adult Great Dane's bed takes up enough room on its own, without taking a litter of, say, ten puppies into account as well. Provided that the premises are warm, dry and clean, and the puppies happy and well social-ised, you shouldn't be too worried.

If you're totally new to puppy buying, why not take someone with you who's done it before? This person will be aware of the correct signs to look out for, and what questions to ask.

With a reputable, caring breeder, be prepared to be questioned yourself. Genuine, responsible dog breeders love their puppies a great deal and will need to be satisfied about their future welfare and the life they are sending them off to live. In fact, it is wise to be extremely cautious of breeders who don't enquire about your circumstances. If they don't care where their puppies are going to spend the rest of their lives, the chances are they won't have cared about any other aspect of their breeding programme either. Reputable breeders will also strictly insist you return the puppy to them should you need to give him up for any reason.

After making friends with the bitch (the friendly one with the 'undercarriage' and desperate expression) and sadly informing her that we would only be taking one of her children, we turned our attention to her puppies. There were eight furry blobs, each one greatly resembling my Grandad, but without the Woodbine and the rolled up copy of the *Beano*. We studied the puppies carefully and made our choice after much consideration. The pup we had chosen was slightly darker than his brothers (just a personal preference). He was also slightly more outgoing than the majority of the litter, although by no means the most extrovert, as we had been warned against picking the 'bossyboots' of the litter, since 'bossyboot' puppies tend to grow into 'bossyboot' dogs: not an ideal choice of character for a first-time Great Dane owner to contend with. We studied our puppy closely to see if he would suit the name that we had chosen for him long before he had even been conceived. He was and still is Hovis, a name that suits him perfectly.

We paid a deposit and the breeder put a small colour-coded cat collar on him to identify which puppy was ours. This was also very useful early training to get him used to wearing a collar, a milestone he barely even noticed. We then arranged visiting rights so we could all get a little more familiar with one another, in preparation for the big day when our little dog would be leaving to come home with us.

While on the initial visit, if you have decided you would like one of the puppies, you can give the breeder a piece of cloth, which he can place in the bitch's bed to pick up smells from her and the other pups. You can then take this piece of cloth when you collect your puppy, and put it with him in his new bed. The smells on it may comfort him through his early, bewildering days in his new environment.

Now you just need to contain yourself until the big day arrives. If you can't manage self-restraint and you've got plenty of cash, get yourself down to the pet shop and spend, spend, spend (see next chapter)! Also, while waiting, use this quiet, peaceful time to go around your house and garden and make it 'puppy proof'. Don't forget to pay particular attention to tucking all electric cables well out of the way. Move all chemicals out of the path of inquisitive noses. Check for gaps small enough for your puppy to squeeze himself into and get stuck, and block them off. And, although the rest of your family will think you're mad and your visitors will possibly attempt to have you committed, try lying on the floor and looking at your house from a puppy's point of view. Remember, puppies have no sense of logic or danger. They don't realise that, if they chew that wire, your home contents insurance premium will increase dramatically next year. And to you it just looks like a tuft of carpet: to your puppy it is a wild, furry creature to be jumped on and tortured until it submits or unravels. Also, if he can get behind the sofa, he may think it's an ideal, secluded place for his toilet. And if he does poo behind your sofa, you can be sure it will only be discovered when Great Aunt Ethel comes for tea. By which time, it will be rock hard and have its own white, furry mohair jacket.

Great Danes shouldn't really be allowed to run up and down the stairs while their bones are still growing and soft, so you might like to get a baby's stair gate. Instead of buying one for this relatively short period of time, perhaps you can persuade a friend who's between children to lend you hers. Don't forget to tell your friend it's for the new puppy though, or you may start being given gifts of booties and bonnets. All of which will look really silly on your new 'baby'.

Now, I've got two thoughts on the subject of cleaning. You can either equip yourself with a pair of rubber gloves and a stack of expensive cleaning products and spend twelve hours a day cleaning up after your puppy, or you can be perfectly normal and compromise a little bit. You can either have a spotlessly clean house, or a Great Dane. You can't have both, and it is therefore pointless even trying, especially if, like Hovis, your puppy is likely to become quite a baggy-faced Dane, as he will almost certainly have a slobber problem.

Decide where you're going to let your puppy eat, sleep and go to the toilet and remember to stick to it. It isn't fair to let him do something in one place one day, then expect him to understand when you change your mind the next day and try to move him. Decide and discuss with the rest of the family which chairs, if any, the puppy will be allowed on. You could also discuss what kind of training methods you are going to use and what the key words will be. These preparations will all go towards helping to avoid any confusion, which could hinder your progress with training after your puppy has arrived.

Why not also use this time to get some Great Dane books and read everything you can on the breed? Visit people who already have one, if you know any. Too much knowledge can't hurt, and if by chance you are put off, then better you discovered now rather than after you've got your dog, when it will be far too late.

While you're at it, don't forget to check your garden. If there are any holes in your hedge or fence, your puppy, with his in-built escape radar system, will find them. Don't forget to check at the very bottom of the hedges, as Danes are quite adept at belly crawling, and can wriggle through what appears to be nothing more than a 5 cm-high gap. I have even heard of older puppies scaling three-metre-high chain link fencing, an accomplishment that would have to be seen to be believed, I think. People might be kind enough to return him to you when he's little, but they won't fancy trying to rugby tackle him much past eight or nine months old, when he weighs about 60 kilos.

All that's left for you to do now is to sit back and survey your nice, clean, orderly home and accept the fact that it isn't going to be like this for quite a while to come, if ever. Console yourself with the knowledge that it can't be that bad, as most people who have had one Great Dane go on to have them again and again. Perhaps, if you take total leave of your senses, you might even have more than one at a time. Now, where did I put the *Yellow Pages*?

PREPARING FOR YOUR PUPPY
(Watch out, purse)

W e were so excited to be almost Dane owners that we had an urge to visit every pet shop that we'd ever heard of and surround ourselves with 'doggy' things. We bought everything our soon-to-be new friend could possibly need, or want. A collar and lead. Various chews to keep his teeth healthy. Furry things he could sleep with to help him settle in. Ropes which act like dental floss. Chews which act like plaque removers. Owners which act like demented, obsessed idiots. You name it, we bought it.

There is a vast array of 'things' for dogs. Some of them are good, some of them useless, some of them even incredibly dangerous and manufactured with the sole purpose of making money. With hindsight, all we should really have bought were: a 'Kong' (this is an almost indestructible rubber toy with an erratic bouncing action, and which dogs love); a thick rope chew, without which one or more of our chair legs might be missing; a tennis ball, only for small puppies (it *must* be discarded before it can fit inside your puppy's mouth and possibly choke him), and a 'Nylabone' chew, again for the sake of the chair legs, and again, make it a large one. Instead we ended up with a bin full of useless toys, which had lasted all of five minutes, each of them carefully designed to appeal to the owners, but only sturdy enough for the gentlest of fluffy kittens.

Obviously, as your puppy grows and wears out these

toys, you'll need to replace them with new ones. Your puppy's tastes will probably change as well and he'll get bored with toys he'd previously thought were great fun. Later on, in Hovis's adolescence, we also found that the 'Frame Ball' and a soft rubber Frisbee were capable of holding his attention for longer than a nanosecond. In fact, with our dog, his Frisbee-phase has lasted right up to the present day. And although he lacks the mouth/eye co-ordination of the majority of normal dogs and rarely manages to catch the very bright luminous yellow dinner-plate-sized object in mid-flight, it doesn't stop his enjoyment of trying. And the fact that it is made from soft rubber means it doesn't hurt his teeth when, on the odd occasion, he finally succeeds in catching it in mid-flight.

On the subject of collars and leads, I feel compelled to add here that I personally do not like choke chains at all, and I can't imagine dogs are very keen on them either. I could perhaps begin to try and see the point of them if they worked, but, on every single instance I have come across one of these horrible weapons, the dog still pulls, just more painfully than if he were on a fixed collar. If you can't train your dog without the need to strangle him, you must be doing it wrong.

One long lead will last for many months, but with collars, no sooner have you buckled up your lovely, shiny new collar on your little puppy, than you find he has outgrown it. Great Dane puppies really do grow at an almost unbelievable rate of knots. For this reason, get into the habit of running your fingers between your puppy's collar and his neck regularly, to check for tightness, and adjust accordingly. I know someone who was almost forced to resort to bolt croppers to remove a choke chain from a dog simply because they had failed to notice how fat its neck had got.

With regard to buying a bed, we just used a variety

of gradually enlarging, easily washable foam pads for Hovis's bed in the beginning. We started off with a relatively small piece to ensure that when he was small he felt cosy and snug, not rattling around in a full-sized bed. We finally ended up with a camp bed mattress folded in half and stuffed in a cover. Great Danes are big, heavy, bony dogs and like to lie on a well padded surface. If forced to lie on hard surfaces, they are prone to getting unsightly, calloused skin on their elbows.

While in the pet shop, if you know what your puppy is being fed, you should get a small supply of this food. Even if you plan to change your puppy's diet, it is best for him (and possibly your floor) if you feed him on what he's familiar with while he's settling in. Then, when you want to change his food, do it gradually. Contrary to what I thought before getting my dog, Great Danes have quite delicate stomachs, and will not hesitate to demonstrate this to you in the most unpleasant way possible.

On the subject of the contents of your dog's stomach, get two poop scoops and a good supply of bags for them. Keep one on a hook next to the lead and one in the glove box in the car. There is never, ever an excuse for not cleaning up after your dog. And yes, I can bang on about the disgusting minority of dog owners forever, with a completely clear conscience, as I have never not cleaned up after my dog has messed in a public place. I have even been commended for doing this 'embarrassing' act. Well, although it's very nice to be praised, I really don't find it embarrassing at all. Cleaning up after your dog should just be considered part of responsible dog ownership, not something to be ashamed of. Besides, nowadays you're likely to get hung, drawn and quartered for letting your dog mess anywhere. Even if you've got every intention of cleaning up after your dog, the looks you will receive whilst he is 'in the act' won't be at all pleasant. Although the true aficionado can always spot the people who have no intention of cleaning their dogs' mess up. They are the ones who hold the lead at arm's length and look the other way, as if adopting this stance would fool the rest of us into thinking that they are not with their dog. If you feel that picking up your dog's poo is beneath you, then, to be perfectly honest, you don't deserve to have a dog.

If you're willing to persevere you can train your puppy to go to the toilet on command. Simply say your key word (ours is 'loo') every time your dog does his business in your garden. Then on your way out of the door for his walk, but before you put the lead on, give him the instruction, i.e. "Go to the loo", and after a short while, or longer if, like Hovis, he's a bit thick, he'll eventually cotton on. This is a situation where you benefit from having a dog who desperately wants to go everywhere with you. If he thinks he can't come until he's 'performed', he'll go every time you tell him to. You must be 100% certain, though, that he understands what it is you want him to do. As with all your training, remember, you are in effect teaching your dog a foreign language. If someone were to say to you, "Sortez les chats", and you weren't French, would you know what it meant? (It's 'Put the cats out', by the way).

Whilst on your spending spree, get your dog a brush. Apart from making him look and probably feel better, from your dog's point of view the act of grooming goes a lot deeper than this. The actual position you take to brush him means that you will be standing over him. This position, plus the fact that in the wild the act of grooming itself is reserved for the top dog in the pack, means that indirectly you are saying to your dog from when he is small and manageable, "I am dominant over you and am allowed to do this to you whenever I want."

Hopefully, he may still remember this when he's bigger than you are.

We'd bought fairly large bowls and, apart from the first few weeks, when we fed Hovis from the cat's bowl, he was happy with these. We chose the heavy ceramic bowls to begin with, as puppies tend to stand in their dinner and tip the lot over on to the floor. Now he's older and a lot taller, we use a bowl stand. This is designed to hold the stainless steel type of bowl. It's much, much better for him if you use a bowl stand when your dog starts getting tall, but you'll feel a bit silly buying one too early, as the stand itself will be bigger than your puppy. For reasons beyond me, these bowl stands aren't available in high street pet shops, but you can get them by mail order through dog magazines, and also from the trade stands at Crufts. They come in two designs, either a metal frame design, or a plastic cylinder-shaped one. Personally, I prefer the plastic cylinder one.

Another good acquisition is a good reference book, because, if you're anything like me, you'll want to refer to it every time your puppy sneezes just to make sure he hasn't been struck down with Kennel Cough, or worse. Start saving up for the entire range of Great Dane books, videos, mugs and teeshirts, as once you've got your Dane, you will buy anything to do with them. Just to put another enormous strain on your pocket, the National Great Dane Rescue sell a large range of quality breed merchandise, and the money goes towards helping less fortunate Danes than yours. Contact them at the address at the end of this book.

Now is also the best time to find yourself a good vet. Don't wait until you need one. The best way of doing this is through personal recommendation. Ask your friends whom they go to, as most people are fiercely protective of their pets and would rather sell their souls to the devil than entrust the health and wellbeing of their animals to just any Tom, Dick or Harry. Having had five cats before we got Hovis meant that we didn't have the worry of wondering if Mr. So-and-So round the corner would be better than Mrs. Such-and-Such up the road. We already had a good vet whom we trusted (and already owed money to).

It might also be worth your while, before getting your puppy, to pay a visit to your vet just to discuss Great Danes, and find out about their general health. Ask him about Bloat, also known as gastric torsion or GDV (Gastric Dilatation Volvulus). This is a very serious, life-threatening condition, which affects large breeds of dogs, including Danes. Sadly, if your dog gets it, he only has a 50% chance of survival, and even that's only if you get him to the vet without delay. Ask your vet to tell you the symptoms to watch out for and any preventive measures you can take. You will probably never see this awful condition, but you should be aware of its existence.

It's well worth insuring your puppy, but shop around before you get him, as there are many different policies and prices to choose from and, after you've collected your puppy, it will completely slip your mind until you receive your first enormous vet's bill. Also, if you try to insure your dog after he has already been treated by the vet for a specific illness, most insurance companies, although they might still insure him, won't insure him against that particular illness, for at least the next twelve months.

When your dog reaches about ten or eleven months old, you'll know his likes and dislikes. You'll know which items were used once and then put away, and which ones were used to destruction. The things he loves, and you use constantly, will be the ones the manufacturers stop making just when yours needs replacing. Now is the time, also, to breathe a sigh of relief, as you will hopefully have gone through the most expensive time of dog ownership. Remember though, above all else, the best things you can provide your dog with are your time, attention and love. These are what he really requires. All the other gadgets, gizmos and toys are fun and entertaining but, at the end of the day, he will destroy them and they'll be thrown in the bin. Without your love, though, he really cannot thrive.

BRINGING YOUR PUPPY HOME
(Preparing for the blitz)

We picked our puppy up on a Sunday. Not because of any religious beliefs about handling puppyfat or a poop scoop on the Sabbath, but because Sundays, in our house at least, are usually calm, quiet days, ideal for settling in a new family member. It's also worth mentioning here that it is much easier to housetrain a puppy in the summer, when doors can be left open and, as the weather is warmer, there is no tendency to rush your puppy so that you can get back inside by the fire.

On the way home from the breeder's, my husband drove the car and I held the little dog on my lap, on a thick towel just in case he was sick. Luckily he wasn't, and remains, to this day, an excellent traveller. This may be because he got used to travelling from day one, as we have always taken him everywhere with us. The only problem we came across was when we changed our car. He didn't like the new one at all. The big advantage though, with being a Great Dane owner is that these dogs will follow you to the ends of the earth. They feel so much part of your family that they don't want to be left behind. You can use this advantage in a possibly daunting situation like getting into the back of a new car. If he sees the rest of 'his' family getting in, he will follow. We have now progressed to a van, which Hovis loves travelling in. He thinks it is his own personal mobile home. I swear I've seen him pulling faces out of the back window, at the drivers following behind.

On 'puppy collection day', we bought some food from the breeder and bundled that, and puppy, into the car. The breeder should also give you a diet sheet explaining what your puppy has been fed on and giving recommendations as to any changes or alterations needed in the future. Be certain to pick up your puppy's pedigree and Kennel Club registration paper at this time as well. My advice is to delay handing your money over until you have been given these documents, and be wary of any breeder who says he will forward the papers on to you, or that they are in the post. There are a handful of breeders who will sell you a puppy which they claim is K.C. registered, but which will turn out not to be, and what's more, there is the possibility that it can never be. These unscrupulous parasites are becoming ever more prevalent, and I speak from first-hand experience. If you're paying for papers, insist on getting them before it's too late. These incredibly irresponsible and irritating people know exactly what they're doing and that, once you've got your puppy home, you won't return him like a faulty television, just because you haven't received his papers. If you do happen to come across a breeder of this ilk, do not hesitate to report him to the Kennel Club and ask your local Trading Standards office to look into his business.

On reaching our house, Hovis took one look at our lovely 'bowling green' lawn, and promptly wee'd on it. We looked on lovingly, politely ignoring the fact that the patch of grass was slowly turning brown before our very eyes. After a short while we thought we'd introduce him to our five cats, who were lying in wait for him in the kitchen. He ran straight up to them with a 'let's be friends' look on his face. They braced themselves with a 'let's not' look on theirs as Hovis plunged head-first into the furry pile. Eighty perfectly sharpened feline claws inserted themselves into the little dog, while twenty ran up the curtains (Toby was, and still is, the original 'scaredy cat'). Extricating himself from his impromptu feline acupuncture session, and unharmed and undeterred, Hovis proceeded to vet his new home with the attitude of 'so many smells, so little time'.

A short while later we thought it proper to offer him his first meal. On examining the diet sheet, which resembled a NASA instruction manual, I lovingly opened and chopped up a packet of tripe; something whose claim to be related to meat is open for debate and, even if is, it looks as though it has been digested once already, and regurgitated. This then had a duck's egg broken over it. Hovis was offered this along with some lamb's milk. He didn't fancy the food, but guzzled the milk down greedily before waddling off to find somewhere to sleep. We showed him to his new bed. We had put a furry toy in the bed and he genuinely seemed to find comfort in this, sleeping on top of it with his face buried in the fur. All in all, he appeared to settle in remarkably quickly. He was left in peace to sleep off his first rush of excitement.

When he woke, we immediately took him outside and put him on the same spot on the lawn where he had been earlier, where he performed like a magician, turning half a pint of lamb's milk into nine pints of wee. He spent the rest of his first day with us intermittently exploring and sleeping.

At night-time we decided, wrongly as things turned out (see later section on 'SLEEPING'), that we wanted him to sleep in our bedroom. We simply took his bed and placed it where we wanted him to sleep, and he obligingly settled down for the night. We automatically woke, like over-anxious new parents, a couple of times during the night and took him outside to the toilet. Now, whether we struck incredibly lucky with Hovis I don't know, but we found toilet training no more difficult than this. The only thing to bear in mind is, although it's tempting, don't keep picking your puppy up and carrying him outside, because he's eventually going to have to learn to get there under his own steam and wait to be let out. But having said that, I suggest that you don't try to rush things.

Let your puppy settle in for a couple of days, then take him to the vet for a check-up, just to make sure he's perfectly healthy. This will probably be the only time in your dog's life that you will be able to carry him in manually and lift him on to the table. Your vet will probably give you a sanity assessment, and your puppy his first injection at this time.

If you haven't done it already, it's also an ideal time to pick your vet's brains. Find out about the best worming and de-fleaing products that are available. You will need large quantities of these for the next 8 years or so. It is worth bearing in mind that if you have cats as well, no matter how much your cat hates your new puppy, it will willingly share its fleas, worms, ear mites etc. with him, whether he wants them or not.

No sooner have I done the rounds of de-fleaing and worming, than one of my squeaky-clean cats will go out and catch a rabbit. Unfortunately I can, on very good authority, inform you that the average wild rabbit is absolutely bouncing with fleas. My cats will then collectively devour half of the aforementioned victim, and either leave the other half in the garden for the dog, or even regurgitate their slimy half and offer to share that with him. Either way, it's revolting and it reintroduces fleas and worms. I feel compelled, therefore to dose my animals every three months in the hope of staying on top of the problem. Make regular worming and de-fleaing a priority. Also make a point of picking up your puppy's mess from the garden, as worms can live in the soil.

Although it's understandable that children will be excited about the new arrival, don't let them persistently mob the puppy. It's very important that he has a bolthole where he can go when he's either tired or when he's just had enough of everyone. Even if it's only a folded-up blanket in the corner of the room, all children must understand that when the puppy goes to his 'sanctuary', he must be left alone and in peace. Some people use a dog 'cage' for this purpose. We had not thought to get one of these, and by the time we did think about it, Hovis was too big to fit in one

Adults also come into the category of well-meaning nuisances to a tired, bewildered puppy. Don't invite everyone you know round to see him on the first day. Consider that he is in a new and frightening world. There will be plenty of time in the days to come for them all to see your new puppy, and to breathe a sigh of relief that he belongs to you, and not them.

It's a source of irritation to every new puppy owner that there is, at the moment, no quick way through the immunisation system. Your dog simply can't go out walking until about two weeks after his final jab, although you can carry him around to let him see his new world. Things are improving, though, with the increasing availability of puppy playgroups. These groups are run by either dog training clubs or vets, and allow your puppy to interact with other puppies and fully vaccinated adult dogs with very little risk of infection. Find out if there is one in your area, as they are a good way of socialising your puppy and letting him know he's a dog and not a human being. If you can't find a puppy class, ask friends with fully inoculated, well behaved dogs to bring them round and introduce them to your puppy.

Just because your puppy isn't allowed out walking in the streets, it doesn't mean you can't still train him. You can begin all the 'Sit!', 'Stay!' type of training in your own home and you can even walk him around with his lead on, either inside your house, or around your garden. You have the added advantage that he can't be too disobedient, as he can't run away too far. Unless, of course, you have a huge garden.

Training can never start too young, but don't expect too much from him: he's only a baby. You wouldn't expect a six-month-old child to recite the entire works of Shakespeare. If you try to work him too hard, he will tire quickly, he will be easily distracted and he will become bored with the whole experience. And once you've lost his attention, it may take some time to get it back, perhaps even several years. Remember to be consistent in your training and don't chop and change key words or hand signals. Danes are very easy dogs to confuse.

It goes without saying that you should never, ever lose your temper with your puppy. This is much easier to say than to put into practice I know, but if you lose your temper with him when he's very young he will lose confidence, and by losing your temper you may end up shouting at him, and if you do shout at him you will frighten him. And there is nothing clever about having a dog which is scared of you.

If you lose your temper and shout at an adolescent Dane, not only will he lose all the respect he had for you, but he will shout back, and, believe me, he can shout much, much louder than you can. What will you do then? For the sake of the limited Neanderthals, who sadly may still be around, I must stress that you should never, under *any* circumstances, ever hit your dog. All you are achieving if you hit him is proving that not only have you failed to train him properly, but you are also an inadequate owner. You are hitting him out of frustration because you couldn't get him to do something by using your voice alone. This is YOUR fault, not his. Go back to the beginning of your training and start all over again, only this time don't rush it. In fact, if you are so quick to hit your dog, give him to someone who deserves him and will appreciate him, as you obviously don't.

Console yourself that these early days are the most testing and sometimes very frustrating times. You will have to deal with toilet training, feeding, and lead work, along with perhaps arguments between your puppy and any existing pets, plus the usual disruption a puppy can cause. But, no matter how difficult you find it, spare a thought for your little dog. He too has to deal with all this, plus the fact that he is new to the world as well. You at least are in familiar circumstances, surrounded by familiar things. He's not.

1. Early days

2.& 3. A quart into a
pint pot.

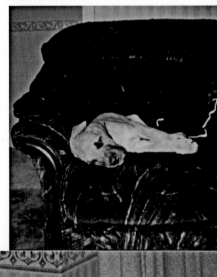

4. & 5. A Great Dane doesn't just
fit discreetly into your house.

. Hovis shows off his paces.

. But watch out for the fly-by!

8. The dignified Dane profile.

9. He will always be there for you.

FEEDING
(Stoking the furnace)

Feeding is the one subject about which, no matter what decisions you have reached, whoever you next talk to will easily convince you that you are doing it all wrong.

I think it can safely be said that the way forward is with dried, complete dog foods. Most people I have spoken to, pet owners, dog breeders and vets alike, all agree on the benefits of these foods. These include storage; the average Great Dane will consume around six cans of 'complete' tinned food per day: have you got the room to store forty-two tins of dog food each week? Then there is the 'food to faeces' ratio. With the good quality brands, the daily amounts needed are relatively small; therefore, less in his stomach equals less on your lawn.

When choosing a complete, dry food, check the guidelines on the packet stating how much of the food the manufacturer recommends that you feed your dog. For a long time I refused to buy the expensive brands, working on the theory that it was a waste of money to pay nearly £40 for a bag of dog food when I could get one for £20. However, on reading the recommended daily amounts required for the £20 sack, I realised I would need to feed more than twice as much as the more 'expensive' ones, because the quality wasn't as good. This proved what false economy the cheap one was.

We were unlucky with our puppy in that he was, in

the beginning, a very fussy eater. When we first brought him home, we had almost made up our minds to get Hovis off the tripe (sadly the choice of food which many breeders still use) and on to something slightly less offensive (coprophagia is almost less offensive than tripe). The decision was helped along not only by our vet, who advised us that tripe was not the best food for a fast-growing puppy, but also by the fact that it took about three months to get rid of the cloud of bluebottles which hung around our bin like local thugs in antici-pation of me throwing more of the revolting stuff away (there is nothing like a binful of green tripe outside in the middle of summer to make you unpopular with the neighbours). It was also assisted by Hovis himself. He'd worked out exactly how to make these strange human-being-type creatures look really silly.

His method was quite simply to stop eating. It was as easy as that. By refusing his food, he could make these humans behave in a very strange manner. His plan went along the lines of: refuse tripe, worried owners then offer tinned food. Refuse tinned food – owners then offer dried food. Refuse dried food – owners then offer something they've slaved over for hours. Refuse everything – owners will then do handstands and somersaults in a vain attempt to get you to eat.

I am slightly ashamed to say that we tried everything, and I mean everything, to persuade our puppy to eat. Apart from buying every single brand of puppy food on the market (both tinned and dry), we tried a whole range of tricks. We tried feeding him by hand, we tried throwing dried food on the garden and letting him forage for it, and we tried holding one of the cats near his bowl to see if it would stir up his natural greed. And I have to say that all of these methods did work – once. If we tried them again, they had no effect whatsoever. Someone did tell me that in the wild the pups' mother would chew the food up and regurgitate it into their mouths, but even I had to draw the line somewhere.

We did notice also, that every mealtime would bring on a bout of hiccups and, although we found these funny, we were concerned enough about them to mention it to the vet on our next visit. Our vet took one look at the perfectly glowing, healthy pup and another at the perfectly paranoid owners, and shared his vet school training, skill and wisdom with us. "This pup is very clever for his age," he said. "Look at how easily he has manipulated you into changing not only his brand and type of food, but the way in which you feed him. This time next week he'll have you preparing him fillet steak while standing on one leg doing the Macarena." He sent us home with instructions to play it cool and not make mealtimes anything special. We were advised to put his food down, sit him out, then about 15-20 minutes later take his food up and offer him nothing else until the next mealtime. The reason for the hiccups was simply excitement, he said. Our little dog was getting excited with our dinnertime fun and games and this was triggering his hiccups. "Calm things down, the hiccups will stop and he will eat," promised our vet. Of course we didn't believe him and, of course – he was right! We have become very observant Great Dane spotters, and it's interesting to note that when you see someone walking a Dane there is usually another small 'terrier type' on the other lead. This dog could be a companion, I suppose, but I'm inclined to wonder if the little dog wasn't obtained for the purpose of encouraging the Dane to eat.

Hard as it may seem, if you are going through a similar experience with your puppy, take the time to remind yourself that no animal in the world is going willingly to starve itself to death. Anorexia doesn't happen in the jungle. Any damage done to your puppy's growth is more likely to happen because of the quality of his food, not the quantity of the meals he chooses to eat.

Don't ever be tempted to feed your puppy cat food. The chances are that he will eat it, but you will be doing him no favours at all. Cat food is designed for cats (and sometimes hedgehogs – unlike bread and milk, but that's another story). Cat food is nutritionally balanced to cater for a cat's body and needs, not a dog's, least of all one of the giant breeds, which really do need the correct balance of food for their extreme rate of growth.

Hovis did go through a very lean phase. He looked like an escapee from Belsen at one point. As an act of desperation, I shamefully confess to putting a variety of things in his dinner in the hope that it would fatten him up. I tried beef suet, dripping, even sugar. All these ingredients did was give him diarrhoea. Every time we needed to go to the vet, for whatever reason, we would ask the same question, "Do you think he's too thin?" and every time the vet would answer with "No." It wasn't until I was told that Great Dane puppies are better off on the lean side as it doesn't put their growing bones and joints under any undue stress, that I was happy with our canine toast rack. I'd been terrified of him being undernourished as I'd read all about growth plates and seen those pictures of the puppies with the bandy legs. What Hovis did do, though, was to grow in spurts. About every two weeks he would be ravenous and eat everything in sight. During these phases you could almost see him getting bigger. After about a week of being a mobile canine dustbin, he would return to being his picky self, only for the cycle to repeat itself two weeks later.

Writing it down now brings it all back. How I worried, needlessly of course! My dog now exceeds the breed standard for both height and weight, and his legs are as straight and sturdy as tree trunks. He eats everything put in front of him, regardless of whether it is supposed to be edible. The only legacy from the difficult months, is his need to have someone staying in the room while he eats. If you leave the room while he's eating, he will follow you. I don't find it an inconvenience to stay with him, though. After the trauma of his early eating habits, it is still a joy to see him devouring his meals with gusto.

It is much better for Great Danes if you don't feed them off the floor; they're far too tall. As soon as it looked as if Hovis was splaying his legs to reach his bowl, we made a wooden stand to fit it into. This first stand lasted quite a long time before it needed replacing with a taller one. If you're really clever at DIY you could make one that you can adjust as your dog grows. Or, to make things really easy, do what we did, and just buy one.

At mealtimes, Hovis likes to perform the 'Great Dane Waltz' (or the Blue Dane-ube!) He will bury his face into his dinner and side step around and around his bowl stand. Since he is fed against a wall, this does limit his actions to performing a semi-circular dance. If fed in the middle of the room, I have no doubt that he would do the complete circuit many times in the course of one meal. All he needs is a couple of pairs of white stilettos and he'd go down a storm in any nightclub, dancing around his handbag.

We found it much more preferable for all concerned to leave the water bowl outside, and this too should be raised. The dog soon learns to ask to go out for a drink and as ours likes to dangle his lips over the edge of the bowl, it stops us from getting the dreaded moat of foam, which would accumulate on the carpet when drinking indoors.

To sum up, my thoughts on feeding are that, providing you are using a good quality food, it doesn't

matter if Mrs. Bloggs round the corner swears by finely
minced Tibetan ox tails, mixed with hand milled
wholemeal flour, with a dash of extra virgin olive oil. If
she wants to spend her days making her dog's food
that's up to her, but tell her you'd like a life instead.
Remember, most breeders succeed with relatively
cheap food, as they have a lot of large canine stomachs
to fill and it would prove very expensive to feed every
dog they own the best quality dried dog food on the
market.

With regard to additives, providing you are feeding
a good quality, complete food, it will need nothing extra.
Complete foods are exactly what they say they are:
complete. If you are going to start adding to your
puppy's food, you will be unbalancing it and besides,
too many additives can do just as much damage to his
bones as a poor diet.

Although it is not exactly an additive, an awful lot of
people (myself included) mix their dog's dry food up
with some liquid. This can either be gravy made from
a very small amount of canned dog food and warm
water, or even just plain water to moisten it a little. If
Hovis is given dry food without any liquid on it, apart
from turning his nose up, I find it tends to make him
cough.

One of the disadvantages of having a fussy eater is
that it does tend to make training a little more difficult.
You can't rely on the bribery and temptation value of
treats. If your dog doesn't respond to food treats, try
using a toy instead.

There are no hard and fast rules about how often
you should feed your dog. It will depend on him, really.
When we first brought Hovis home, he was on four
meals a day. He gradually cut these down on his own,
until at about seven months he was on just two. Now,
at just over a year and a half old, he is still on two meals

a day, although some dogs at this age have cut even this down to just one meal a day. I would rather feed Hovis twice a day, as the current opinion is that giving one large meal daily may contribute to the risk of your dog getting bloat (GDV), and anything which lessens the risk of my dog getting this high-mortality-rate condition can only be a good thing.

Our dog chooses to make breakfast his smallest meal, while opting to stuff his face totally in the early evening. When deciding what times to feed your dog, bear in mind that Great Danes shouldn't be exercised for at least an hour after they've eaten. Again, this is because of the dreaded Bloat (this word will haunt you for your entire Dane-owning life).

Try not to give your dog titbits all day. There is a curious human condition, which compels us to think that if our pets are eating, they must be happy. Perhaps, on the face of it, this seems to be true. However, in the long run we are doing them no favours at all. You will end up with an overweight, unfit and unhealthy dog, and you will have taught him to be greedy, thereby making him not only unpleasant to have around, but also a nuisance. There can be no worse sight than a dog scrounging at the table. *You* may find this cute and appealing, but you can be 100% certain that your dinner guests won't.

Great Danes, on the whole, are naturally lean dogs, although I have come across one or two fat ones in the past. They don't seem to carry fat very well and the whole 'look' of the Great Dane is spoiled if he is carrying too much excess baggage. Having said all that, we do give Hovis treats, but they aren't an entitlement. He knows he has to earn them. Luckily for us, he is naturally a thin dog and doesn't carry an ounce of extra fat at all. I just wish I could say the same about myself.

EXERCISING
(Get the saddle ready)

I bet he takes a lot of walking." Read that statement aloud lots of times, practice gritting your teeth and pretending you've never heard it before and it might help to prepare you for the countless times you are going to hear it in the future.

Perfectly 'normal' people, on seeing your Dane, switch from being astute, rational human beings into robots and can't seem to stop themselves saying one of these phrases: "Look at the size of his feet" – although this is usually reserved for the younger puppy. "I bet he eats a lot" (grit your teeth) and "I bet he takes a lot of walking" (and smile). Just when you've congratulated yourself on managing not to say, "Oh how very funny, I've never heard that one before," they'll come out with that old side-splitting rib tickler, "You could put a saddle on that and ride it home." Only then can you feel free to guffaw away at their very original sense of humour. Joking apart, try to smile politely: they mean well.

When you first take your puppy out, you may actually feel cheated that you can't take him on great, long, rambling walks. You may have had visions of you and your faithful hound disappearing off to the horizon, but you just can't do this at the beginning. This is because of his soft bones. Because of the rate of growth achieved in the early stages, too much walking can actually damage his legs. Better to use the early months for lead training and manners rather than for hiking any great distance.

Our dog was around 10 months old before he had any stamina to speak of. As with any kind of fitness training, we built up his exercise gradually. Can you imagine the problem of tiring him out so much that you have to carry him home? People could then come up to your dog and say to him, "You could put a saddle on that and ride it home."

In an ideal world, you should let your dog have both roadwork to keep his claws short and teach him manners, and a free run. In my opinion there is no greater sight than a Great Dane running loose in an enclosed field. Mind you, catching a Great Dane running loose, even in an enclosed field, is another thing. And apart from when they're puppies and look as if they're made of rubber – although this in itself is an endearing characteristic – they have the most enchanting paces of any dog I've ever seen. Watching one running free shows you exactly why he is the 'Apollo of dogs'. Danes are pure hairy poetry in motion.

Remember, though, that young Danes sometimes find it very amusing deliberately to knock you over. You will learn the art of side-stepping your dog at the last minute as he gallops towards you, but don't forget to tell the other dog walkers who will invariably want to stand and talk to you about him. You will soon learn who 'knows' Danes, as they will partner you in the Great Dane Shuffle.

You should find though, that as he gets older, he will be less inclined actually to knock you over. Instead, he will perform what is known in our house as a 'fly-by'. This manoeuvre begins like the standard knock down, but instead of slamming into you and bowling you over, your dog will just skim the side of your legs. Unfortunately, you won't know whether he's going for a fly-by or the full-blown knock down, until it's too late.

As for lead work, our dog would never (and still

doesn't) truly walk to heel. He always likes to walk just a little in front. This appears to be a characteristic with Great Danes as I've seen it many times with other people's. And, although we did attend dog-training classes, Hovis did not distinguish himself there. He would walk nicely for a while, then seem to forget himself and gradually inch his way further and further in front. He also had a manic obsession with other dogs. When passing them, he would wait until we were alongside, then lunge at them. He didn't mean them any harm, he was just trying to have a high-speed sniff and say, 'hello'. The day he tipped the scales at more than me and tried his lunging trick, almost removing my arm from its socket, I realised that he knew that he was stronger than I was. For this reason, and the constant nagging of "Heel, heel," I realised that, due to the Great Dane's naturally short life span, his time with us was going to be brief enough, without us spending it arguing over lead work. I went out and bought a Halti.

Now, Halti's work. Let this be said straight away. They are also a very easy way out. Personally, I like to take the easy way out. If you want to be a martyr, then that's entirely up to you. I know exactly how you feel, as every time I put on my dog's Halti I still feel guilty that I am taking the easy option instead of training my dog 'properly'. However, I love my dog and any time spent nagging at him, is time spent not enjoying him. I do still train him, but we both understand that when the Halti is on, the lunging stops, the inching in front stops and no thought of pulling on the lead even enters his head. Be warned though, that there are still a limited number of people who aren't familiar with the head collar type of dog lead and will think your dog is wearing a muzzle. Because of this, they will either cross over to the other side of the road to avoid being torn limb from limb, or they will give you a look of utter contempt because they just know that you are secretly training your dog for the seedy underworld of dog fighting.

I would like to add that, along with the Halti, there is another head collar type of gadget which you might find works better. This one is called the Gentle Leader. There was a time, when Hovis was a bit of a fidget, that we found this one preferable to the Halti, as it does not ride up into the dog's eyes, as the Halti can. Now he behaves like a perfect gentleman on the lead, we can use either. We find keeping one in the car and one in the house covers you for most situations. There is nothing like a badly behaved Great Dane for making you look stupid.

There are a variety of harnesses which go around your dog's neck and body, but I can't comment on any of these, as I've not tried them personally. I do have a friend with a Dane who uses one, but every time I see her holding it up in the air at arm's length like a dead octopus, trying to work out which way up it goes, which strap goes where, I think to myself, why bother? In fact, the last time I saw her juggling with it, she told me that she was thinking of disposing of it in favour of a Halti or Gentle Leader herself. Perhaps she could use it for bringing down steers on the pampas. I'm sure they must have a good use, I just haven't worked out what it is yet.

Don't ever worry that you might not be giving your dog enough exercise. He will let you know if you are not taking him out enough by doing the 'wall of death' around your house or garden until you realise he has some energy left that he'd like to get rid of. Having said that, even when he's getting plenty of exercise, occasionally, apparently just for the fun of it, Hovis will tuck his tail right under his bum and take off round the garden ducking and diving like a thing possessed. We've just turfed our lawn for the second time since Hovis came to live with us just over 18 months ago on account of the 'track' he's made when carrying out this activity (yes, really).

The intelligence of Great Danes is open to question. Most articles I've read on the breed claim they are intelligent, yet everybody I've spoken to who owns one or more of these dogs admits that they are a little mentally challenged to say the least. I'll stand up and be counted. I'll openly say out loud that my dog is definitely one sandwich short of a picnic. Perhaps the well-meaning people who write these articles think that we will only give a particular breed of dog a good home if he is a member of MENSA. But because he's a bit thick, I actually love my dog all the more. Perhaps I feel protective towards him because he's a dunce. The only real drawback I've come across is that training can be a little more difficult with a Dane, compared to a dog that has more than four brain cells. You may need to say "sit" three or four times with a normal dog before you get a response; with a Dane, you may need to say it for three or four years.

To get back to the subject of exercising your dog: when you come back from a particularly strenuous bout, feel his feet. If he's had a good run and is quite warm, his feet will be all soft and clammy. There's no particular reason to do this other than the fact that they feel very funny.

Please, please, please don't become one of those stupid people who think it's really clever to walk their dogs along the pavements without a lead on. I don't know what they're trying to prove by indulging in this potentially dangerous activity. I think they are convinced that the message they are giving out is, "Look at me, my dog loves me so much that he will walk with me of his own free will." Big deal! What they are actually saying is, "Look at me, I don't give a hoot whether my dog gets run over or not." As well as the huge risk, not only to your dog's life – you might think you know your dog, but remember he is a living, breathing creature, and this alone makes him unpredictable – but to the lives of others, it's also worth remembering that it is, in most places, illegal.

As your dog gets older, his energy levels will be a little more sporadic than in his earlier months. Some days Hovis will go bonkers when let off the lead, but on others he will be happy just to plod along enjoying the smells. This doesn't mean your dog will let you get away with cutting down on his walks. He will still need to be exercised just as much as before, it's just that the tone of his walks will change. His manners will vary in a similar way. Some days he will walk beautifully on his lead, and on others he will be all over the place, standing on your toes, weaving about, wanting to sniff every lamp-post.

I strongly believe that it's not just the physical side of his walk that the dog enjoys, although watching Hovis going bonkers proves it is an important factor. I think, to a large degree, it is the mental exercise he craves also. Sometimes Hovis will be absolutely shattered after just spending a lot of time travelling in the van or pottering around the garden. His brain seems to get tired, as if it has been asked to absorb too much information.

On the whole, the fully adult Great Dane is quite a lazy dog. Although he will happily accompany you on long walks if you want him to, he is just as happy to lie in his comfortable, warm bed on a cold, winter's day. This doesn't mean you can skimp on his walks, though, if *he* really feels like a walk; he will become very persistent in his quest to get you to take him out, constantly leaping up with an air of expectation every time you so much as look at him until, driven nearly insane, you will escort him to the nearest field. However, when you feel like a walk and he doesn't, he will give you that Dane look of utter contempt and possibly pass you your coat on his way back to his cosy bed.

Hovis absolutely hates the cold, but he especially cannot stand the rain and will do anything within his power to escape going out in it. Aside from making exercising very difficult, this also proves awkward last thing at night when you try to get him to go out to the toilet before going to bed. On several occasions I have even had to resort to physical methods. This usually starts off quite harmlessly with me opening the door and inviting Hovis to go outside. He'll take one look at the rain and politely decline my invitation. I will then advise him that it is in his best interests to go out. He will make the token gesture of poking his nose out of the door to have a closer look at the rain and then shift into reverse, and run backwards back into the warmth of the house.

By this time, it is beginning to get a little draughty and my patience is wearing thin. I will give him one last chance by instructing him in what I kid myself is a stern voice, to go to the loo, before placing myself at the rear end of the big baby, planting a hand on either side of his bottom, and pushing. He has cottoned on to this now so he will have anticipated my next move and braced himself ~~in read~~iness for the big shove. It is possible to push him a little way, but the moment his face is more than four millimetres out of the door, and his nose registers the change in both the air temperature and humidity, his body will concertina and then sink to the floor.

Changing ends will have no effect, apart from placing me closer to the open door than I want to be. But if I do manage to grab his collar and pull, this just results in dragging all the loose skin up his neck, over his ears and on to his face, making him look like an overgrown, underfed Shar-Pei.

Eventually, victory will be momentarily mine and Hovis will tiptoe outside to his post, where he will lift his leg not more than two inches off the ground. From this position, he will pull a face which is meant to con me into thinking he is 'performing', then come scuttling back inside to the comfort of his bed, leaving a trail of muddy wet footprints which, if left until the morning, will set like concrete and require twice as much work to remove them.

Your choice of free exercise obviously will have to be governed by access. As a Great Dane owner, you can only really use either open fields, well away from roads, or fields designated as bridle ways. Unless it has a gate which opens, a stile leading into a field is as good as a brick wall. A Dane has neither the intelligence to work out how to get his bulk over a stile, nor the agility to practise the manoeuvre should he ever manage to work it out.

To sum up exercising and training, I would say: don't over exercise your young dog, you will tire him out and too much exercise isn't good for his soft bones. Be sure to teach him general manners while on the lead and, equally important, teach him to come back when you call him. There are a multitude of books available whose authors are much better qualified in dog training than I am. If you want to have a highly trained dog that jumps through hoops every time you ask him, or watches your every move in anticipation of a command, you will need to read these books so that you can teach yourself to teach your dog.

Bear in mind, that all the books in the world can't change the fact that what you own is a Great Dane, not a Border Collie. When did you last see a Great Dane rounding up sheep, or carrying out obedience work?

Make allowances for the large amount of empty space between his ears. Thankfully, I personally do not like to see a fawning, submissive over-trained dog of any breed. Although I always describe my dog as very highly trained; just not in English!

PLAYING GAMES
(Being a spoilsport)

It is worth noting that from the moment you bring your tiny, innocent bundle of joy home, the games you play in your Dane's life can go a long way to influencing the personality he ends up with.

With a dog as large as a Great Dane, it is absolutely vital from the start that you are the boss, and that the dog knows this.

Being the boss doesn't mean using threatening behaviour, force or physical violence on your dog. Although they can sometimes resemble bumbling buffoons, Great Danes are an extremely sensitive breed. They dislike even being told off, and will go to great lengths to show you that they are sorry if they have been naughty. When shown even just displeasure, Hovis manages to make his head into the shape of a 'deerstalker' hat, while at the same time puckering his baggy lips and wriggling his body around like a sidewinder snake. This is known in our house as 'having his hat on'. He will do this even before you realise he has done anything wrong, like hiding something, be it a sock, tea towel or worse in his huge soggy mouth, thereby completely giving the game away, leaving you just to roll up your sleeve and delve in and find it.

I am a strong believer in getting down on the floor and playing with your dog. Most dogs love a bit of rough and tumble. However, you must decide when the game is over, and stick to it. Don't let your dog hassle you into playing any game for longer than you want to. You have to learn to be a spoilsport and have enough control to 'take your ball home' whenever you like. Remember that brute force won't get you anywhere with a dog that's bigger and perhaps heavier than you are.

This same principle applies to all tug-of-war games. You decide when to play, for how long, and when to finish, and you must win most of them. This is easier said than done when an older, larger puppy weighing around 60 kilos still enjoys this game. You can pull each other around for as long as you want, but you must have adequate control over your dog to be able to make him drop the toy when you have decided to end the game. It's only fair to let him win occasionally, as he will be very reluctant to play if he doesn't think he's at least in with a sporting chance. You'll be thankful for the time you spent over training in the early days. My 12-year-old son does play tug-of-war games with Hovis, but only when I am nearby to grab on to him when he's had enough, as he doesn't have as much verbal control over Hovis as he should. The neighbours must wonder what on earth is going on, watching both of us being swung around the garden.

If you do find yourself unable to make your dog drop the toy, it may help if you can get him to sit first. This will give you a slight advantage over him. If you can't even get him to sit then you've had it. You'll just have to give in gracefully, and make sure you win the next one.

If you let your dog try to control your games, it can inflate his ego too much, which may lead to him making a stand at controlling other aspects of your lives as well. Be alert to any signs of him becoming pushy. Don't always stroke him when he asks you – he may come to demand it. Sometimes, when he nuzzles you, look the other way or fold your arms. And never, ever let him barge through doors before you. Tell him to wait while you go through first, then allow him to follow. Don't let him scrounge for food when you are eating – he might start stealing it. This last point is much easier said than done, and I have to confess to sometimes being just as guilty as everyone else at slipping my dog the odd crisp, or ten.

All these details may seem trivial to you and me, but to a dog they are subtle, but vital, doggy clues as to who's in charge.

Another seemingly harmless but potentially challenging pursuit is the chasing game. Hovis loves to chase us around the garden. This in itself is fine, apart from the fact that he has learnt that, if he hooks his front leg around ours, we fall over. At speed! It is not advisable to reverse this game, though, (the chasing, not the tripping up) as you may be opening yourself up to problems with recalling your dog at other times. Also, if you ever need to grab your dog in an emergency, he might think it great fun to run away then as well, possibly putting himself at risk.

Hovis sometimes likes to play the 'barking game'. He's made his own rules up for this one. It consists of standing about three inches away from you and barking constantly and repetitively. He seems literally to like the sound of his own voice and will go into a kind of trance listening to it. He also seems to use this time to practice his barks, and will vary the pitch and tone while appearing to listen to the results. It is quite possible to slip out from under his nose, make a cup of tea and return to your seat without him even realising that you've gone. Luckily, I have extremely understanding neighbours.

You shouldn't play any biting games with your dog (it's really hard getting the fur out of your teeth). It may seem like harmless fun when your dog is small, but

how are you going to stop him when he's older? Even
the most gentle-mannered Dane can get carried away
when he's excited and possibly cause you serious
damage. He may show an abundance of remorse afterwards, but that's not much use to you when you're down
the local Accident and Emergency department having
your stitches put in. It's really not worth the risk of
being bitten.

Be careful, too, of playing any rough-and-tumble
games with a larger puppy while sitting or lying on the
floor. From this (disad)vantage point your puppy can
very easily overpower you. He'll probably only acci-
dentally stick his huge, camel-like foot in your face, but
it hurts like mad and the claws go up your nose and in
your eye.

You'll notice that as your Dane approaches his first
birthday he will calm down considerably. He'll still be
game for a laugh, but he should be easier to stop when
you've had enough. Although Hovis still likes to chase
after things thrown for him while out in the field, he is
more interested in rummaging in the hedgerows now
he's older and supposedly wiser. He has even caught
the odd rabbit and brought it back to me unharmed.
Sometimes, he does still get the devil in him and go
absolutely bonkers. When particularly possessed he
will take off around and around the field, tail tucked
under him, like a bat out of hell.

Beware of your older Dane who wants to play vigor-
ous, outdoor games when you don't. If you're in the
mood just to stroll around the perimeter of the field
while letting your dog amuse himself, but he wants
some fun and games, he will try everything in his power
to get you to play. Until we taught him better manners,
Hovis had a particular technique. To begin with, he
would run around you in circles to get your attention.
If you ignored this behaviour, he would begin to spring

into the air while still circling you. From here, he would progress to grabbing your arm or foot. If your dog also uses these tactics, be warned that once this stage has been reached, you ignore him at your peril. It is in your best interest to throw him a toy or get out of his way. If you dare to turn your back on him he will hurl himself with great force at the upper part of your body, attempting to slam you with his chest. If you're not too badly winded, you will probably be so taken aback by this most un-gentlemanlike behaviour, that you will be momentarily stunned. On regaining your composure, any attempt to tell him off will result in him springing up and down and circling you just out of your reach.

If your dog does try this behaviour with you, put a stop to it straight away. Not only is it a very bossy way for your dog to gain attention, it also has the potential of being very damaging to not only your health, but his as well, as your immediate reaction on recovery will be the urge to slap him stupid. Count to three and repeat the phrase, "I must not smack my dog," over and over until you believe it – this could take a while! The way to teach him not to perform his body slam is immediately to put his lead on and make him walk to heel. Even though your dog, like mine, may be a little lacking in the brains department, he will soon learn that every time he does this he has to go back on his lead. How do you achieve this? Well, we used to shout Hovis's name in a pretend angry voice, and he seemed to realise it was in his best interests to come; then we'd put his Halti on and regain control, composure and credibility.

Don't be tempted to throw sticks for your dog. Most vets could probably regale you with stories of the injuries they have treated caused by sticks becoming either wedged inside the dog's mouth, or even impaled through the throat. Be alert also to the dangers of dogs getting balls lodged in their throats and blocking their windpipes. I have heard several stories of this happening and the dogs actually dying in front of their owners. Although attempts were made to retrieve the ball, it had become so firmly lodged in the back of the throat that there was no space around it to get a grip with the fingers. Although the risk of either of these accidents happening is small, to me it is still a risk I'd rather not take. There are enough safe toys on the market for my dog to enjoy.

Have fun with your dog but remember that you are the 'pack leader'. It's up to you to decide which games to play, how long for, and to take the toys off him when you've decided you've had enough. He won't take offence: he's only a dog.

SLEEPING
(A quart into a pint pot)

When we picked our puppy up, we had already decided that we wanted him to sleep in our bedroom with us. I'll come clean now and say that for a dog with the personality that Hovis had back then, this was totally the wrong decision (I'll explain in more horrifying detail later).

As we were aware that Hovis was going to grow at roughly the speed of Thrust, and we didn't want him to be rattling around in a full sized bed while he was a small puppy, we didn't go out and buy a proper bed for him at first. We used a selection of gradually enlarging thick foam pads. As he grew, so did his bed. Luckily these pads were washable as, in spite of everything I'd read about dogs to the contrary, which stated categorically that a dog won't do this, Hovis actually wee'd in his bed on a couple of occasions. Admittedly, he was very young and silly, and he did have the decency to look embarrassed afterwards, but he still did it, and so might yours.

By the time he was about eight months old and well out of the wee-ing the bed stage, we managed to get hold of an old camp bed mattress which we folded in half and stitched the edges together to pin it down. This was then stuffed into a washable cover (just in case of any more accidents). It makes a lovely dense bed for a lovely dense dog, and is small enough to fit into the corner of the kitchen, but large enough for Hovis and a couple of cats to spend the night on. A piece of thick foam cut to size would be just as good.

When we're all relaxing, watching TV in the living room, Hovis manages to squeeze himself into an armchair. We decided when we first got him that he wasn't to be allowed on all the furniture at will, but we selected one chair which he could have as his own. A seven-foot-long dog shoe-horning himself into a two-foot space has to be seen to be believed. A Great Dane asleep on an average sized armchair is living proof that you can get a quart into a pint pot. And don't worry about him, he must be comfortable or he would move. This seating arrangement works well for us, and Hovis understands that just because he's allowed on 'his' chair, it does not mean he is allowed to get on any of the others. However, this does not stop him from occasionally reversing onto your lap when there is a particularly riveting programme on the television. His current favourite is 'Pet Rescue'. As soon as he hears the music he puts his feet up and settles down to watch how the other half live.

Due to problems with destruction (see the chapter, 'Your Dog On His Own'), when Hovis was about six months old, we were advised to get him out of our bedroom and make him sleep in the kitchen. As we had always allowed him to sleep in the bedroom with us, we were anticipating major problems in moving him to our chosen spot. But, by gradually moving his bed away from ours, on to the landing, then down to the bottom of the stairs, until finally arriving at this designated place, we achieved this in around eight days. Hovis is perfectly happy sleeping downstairs and moving him out of our room helped a great deal toward curing the problems we were having with his destructiveness. But, with hindsight, although we did find it relatively easy to move him, it would have been a lot easier and kinder to have never let him taste the good life and sleep upstairs in the first place. Hindsight is a truly wonderful thing!

During the evening, our dog will sleep in a selection of areas and styles. One minute he will be curled up tightly on his chair, with his nose stuck up his backside, the next he will be stretched out upside-down looking like a 60kg oven-ready chicken sprawled along the bottom of the sofa. He will even sleep standing up dribbling if you're rubbing the inside of his front leg at the time. Be warned, though, on the practice of rubbing his leg, as once your dog has a taste for this, and knows you're prepared to be his own personal masseur and pander to him in this manner, you won't be allowed to stop. Every time your aching fingers come to a standstill, he will tickle them with his 'flaps' just to get them moving, and if this doesn't work, he will snuffle around your hand with his very cold, wet nose like a truffling pig, until you're forced to restart.

When your dog is asleep, be prepared for some of the strangest noises you're ever going to hear. These sounds vary from growling and barking, to high pitched guinea pig-like squeaks. Hovis makes all these noises and more, and I've sworn that one day I'm going to frighten the life out of him by recording them and playing them back to him. Along with these noises, his legs will pedal as he takes on Linford Christie in his dreams, and goes a few rounds with Prince Naseem Hamid for good measure. Even when he appears to be lying totally still, on close inspection his dewclaws will be twitching away as if he's attempting to thumb a lift. I've come to the conclusion that the reason he sleeps so much is because he's so tired when he wakes up, that he needs some repose to get over it.

When he's feeling especially tired, Hovis doesn't so much arrange himself in a sleeping position, as drop like a stone from wherever he is standing at the time.

If this happens to be above your foot, or small child, then so be it, it's all immaterial to him. There will be no stopping him. If you watch him closely, you may just catch his legs beginning to buckle, giraffe-like, but usually he will go down with very little warning. Once he's down there is not a great deal you can do about it other than attempt to pull your foot, or purple-faced child, from under his dead weight.

Sometimes, when the mood takes him, Hovis will pretend he's about to go to sleep and assume the position of a play-bow-type, pre-sleep stretch[1]. From this position he will do one of two things. He will either begin the biggest yawn possible, almost reaching the stage of having a flip-top head. On completion of this yawn, he will have totally forgotten what he was going to do next. He will therefore remain in this position for some time, appearing, to all intents and purposes, to be mooning at the world. Or he will break wind in the loudest, most shameless manner possible, leaving you, depending on which type of visitors you have with you at the time, either to go scarlet with embarrassment as you pass the Rich Tea biscuits, or punch the air with a cry of "Go on my son, fart for England!"

Some dogs, and Hovis is one of these, have perfected the art of sleeping with their eyes open. He doesn't even do this in the half-lidded manner adopted by the amateurs. He will have both of his eyes wide open, and it's not until you get down on your hands and knees and peer into them, that you can tell that although his lights are on, he's most definitely not in.

Never wake a young puppy when he's asleep. Young puppies, like young babies, need as much sleep as they can get. Place his bed out of the way of 'traffic' and leave him in peace. Even when he's older, you should never really need to wake your dog. If he's only semi-sleeping, the slightest noise, from either a burglar or someone getting his lead, will wake him in an instant. With Hovis, the word 'chocolate', even if spoken so quietly that it is inaudible to bats, will wake him from what appears to be a brain-stem-death coma. If your dog is in genuine deep sleep, leave him be, and don't let children pester him. Just as some humans are a bit cranky when woken, so are some dogs. The difference with dogs is that they can't have a cup of coffee and a cigarette. If your dog is prone to crabbiness, just give him a couple of minutes to gather his thoughts and plan his next manoeuvre.

CHANGING SHAPES
(From 0-75 in nine months)

This chapter has nothing to do with Australian imports into the British line of the Great Dane. This chapter has nothing to do with introducing which champion stud dog to which breeding bitch. This chapter isn't even about the way the Great Dane of the 1990s has changed from the Great Dane of the 1920s. It is purely to let you know that the puppy you take home at about eight or ten weeks old bears not one iota of resemblance to the dog you will have in the end. He will literally go from a round, furry blob to at least 75 cm at the shoulder in about nine months.

Our dog looked like the proverbial 'bulldog chewing a wasp' when we brought him home. Now, though, he bears an uncanny resemblance to a painting on which water has been spilled. His face looks as if it is steadily slipping off. He has quite large ears, and is what some breeders would call a 'lippy' Dane. That is, he has large, droopy lips, or, as we like to call them, his flaps. He also has baggy eyes and a baggy neck. He sounds atrocious I know, but it all seems to fit together quite well into a surprisingly handsome 'package'.

You will notice a huge variation in the facial characteristics of every Great Dane you see from now on, and shortly after becoming a Dane owner you will find that you can tell the difference between a dog and a bitch without looking like you're playing Twister. You'll see that some bitches are truly beautiful, and some dogs proud and handsome. On the other hand, you will also see some that really are as ugly as a bag of spanners. Even the ugly ones are usually so ugly they're adorable.

Personally, I much prefer the tighter faced Danes, but Hovis has such baggy flaps that they spread out around him like a sort of furry Elizabethan ruff while he is sleeping. Kittens and even other puppies have used them for swinging on. I love him to death though and wouldn't swap him for the world. When we first went to see him in the litter, we couldn't tell just by looking at the puppies to what extent their flaps would droop. We did see his mother, so had a rough idea, but never saw the father. Had we seen the dad, we would have been better able to gauge the 'completed' general appearance of our dog. But providing you don't want your dog for breeding or showing purposes, whatever he looks like you'll still love him.

Apart from a Great Dane's knees, which are huge, there is nothing really outstanding about them as puppies. I think all puppies look pretty similar when they're very small: it's only as they grow that the different characteristics begin to appear. It amazes me that Great Danes, as very young puppies, are similar in size to most other breeds. Before we began looking for Hovis, I had envisioned visiting kennels full of puppies the size of young foals gallivanting around. We did visit a breeder who had hung on to some puppies and who let them out each day for exercise in a field. From a distance they resembled gangly lambs skipping about and leaping over one another.

When you first get your puppy, he will be roughly the shape of a slug. From this, he will go through various stages in his relentless march to adulthood. These stages include looking like a dodgem car, a camel, and a moose, before finally reaching, at about one year of age, almost his correct shape. He will continue to grow

for about another year, but with nowhere near the speed
he has demonstrated up to now. A lot of this growing
will be outwards as opposed to upwards; although he
will by no means have reached his ultimate height, he
won't be shooting up as quickly as he did in his first
year. He will develop 'rubber stoppers' on both his
elbows and his hocks. I gather that these stoppers are
nature's way of providing a little cushioning for when
your dog is lying down. All he needs is a matching
helmet and you could be mistaken for thinking he
is fully kitted out in the latest trendy skateboarding
gear.

You will notice him filling out after his first birthday.
This will carry the bonus of making his knees fit
the rest of him. And also, by the age of around twelve
months, you should stop hearing comments like, "Look
at the size of his feet," but don't breathe a sigh of relief
yet as this will be replaced with, "Look at the size of
that dog." On the positive side though, for every ten
people who can't resist commenting on his size alone,
one person will notice his beauty as well, and tell you,
and your heart will swell with pride.

One characteristic, which will stay with him throughout his journey from blob to moose, will be his very
prominent leg veins, wrapping around the bones of each
of his legs. Some squeamish people find these veins
horrible. I find them rather funny, a bit like a design
fault, as if nature couldn't be bothered to tuck its wiring
out of sight.

As you look at your canine blob, take note of his nice
uniform fur pattern. As small puppies, Great Danes
are covered in a smooth blanket of hair. As they get
older, they start to develop 'seams'. One set of seams
will start just under his earflaps; they will head down
his throat and towards his chest where they will just
fizzle out. The other set will appear, almost overnight,

on his bottom. This set resembles a swirly, rosette shape, a little like a handlebar moustache glued on to his rear end.

On the subject of the rear end, even this changes shape. From a normal, rounded puppy bottom, at about four months of age Hovis developed what we call his 'hamster bum'. This pointed bottom resembled that of a male hamster so much, that the name has stuck, even though, with advancing age and weight, his bottom has gone on to round off slightly. Hovis's favourite game used to be 'Tweak My Hamster Bum While Making A Noise Like A Duck'. Sadly, now he thinks he's grown up, if you tweak his hamster bum he looks over his shoulder, and down his nose at you as if you are some kind of pervert. On speaking to other Dane owners about their dogs' bums (well, it makes a change from the weather), I've been told that not all Danes get the hamster bum, and some glide through adolescence with a perfectly rounded posterior.

All puppies go through the stage where their ears look far too big for their heads and, although the German Shepherd has pretty well cornered the market on this one, the Great Dane is no exception. The size of the ears is usually owing to a breeder's personal preference. Some breeders like the large ones, others will only breed dogs with the smaller ears. As a rule of thumb, if both of your puppy's parents had small ears, there's a fair chance your dog won't end up looking like Dumbo. Ear carriage can also either enhance or completely spoil a dog's appearance. I remember seeing a stunning black bitch once, who was beautiful in every way, until you got to her ears. Not only were they tiny, which she might just have got away with, but they were perched on the very top of her head and carried 'fly-away' style. These ears spoiled the whole appearance of this otherwise gorgeous bitch.

Although Hovis has ears which are well within the acceptable range, he does tend to look more than a little elephantine. He also looks incredibly comical when standing in a crosswind.

YOUR DOG ON HIS OWN
(Batten down the hatches)

This chapter really hits me where it hurts as, for a short while, Hovis was the world's biggest brat whenever he was left at home on his own. Although he was only ever left for a maximum of two hours, in those two hours he could do more damage than Hurricane Hugo passing through in a bad mood.

Unbeknown to us at the time, a great deal of the problem was our fault. We had unwittingly turned our young dog into a hanging-on-the-apron-strings-spoilt-child-type-puppy. Our major mistake was that when we first got him, we were touched by the fact that he loved us so much he wanted to go everywhere and do everything with us. He would follow us constantly around the house and garden, never leaving our ankles for a moment. He would follow us to the toilet and wait outside the door. Then when we went to bed, we would take his bed up with us and put it next to ours, and there he would lie until morning.

This idyllic picture was shattered when one day I'd gone out, shutting Hovis in the kitchen, as I had on several occasions before without any trouble. However, on this day he decided that he was bored and he didn't like it on his own any more, thank you very much.

I will never, for as long as I live, forget the scene which met me on my return. Hovis had destroyed everything in the kitchen that he could reach. As he was about six months old at the time, and therefore quite tall, that narrowed it down to everything except the light bulbs. I don't know what triggered him off, and at the time I didn't much care. All I knew was that where I'd once had a kitchen, I now had Hiroshima. It was total devastation. I was even too shocked to be angry. His total score on that first occasion was:

   1 Door mat
   3 Newspapers (unread)
   2 Houseplants (variegated)
  36 Colour photos & negatives (of himself)
   1 Draining board mat
   1 Two-litre bottle of orange squash
   2 Bottles of lemonade (kicked around until really
     fizzy, then punctured and sprayed everywhere)
   1 Postcard from Singapore
   1 National Lottery ticket (with the potential
     earning power of £10,000,000)
   1 Tax demand (it wasn't all bad)
   1 Money-off coupon for 'Toaster Pockets'
     (perhaps it's looking better)

All of the above were left in varying stages of demolition on the floor. First, I could not believe my eyes, and then I could not believe that our cute, loveable, innocent little puppy would do this to us. But he had, and would continue to do so every single time we went out and dared to leave him at home. I would like to take this opportunity to point out, in my own defence, that it was a reasonably tidy kitchen to start with and these items had been put away in their respective places, and not left out under his nose to tempt him.

On one spree, he also managed to add to his grand total:

6 Cactus plants
1 Electric kettle
1 Bread bin
and a postcard from Indonesia

I feel his cactus plant trick is worth a mention in its own right, as it was almost a work of complete genius. Hovis had somehow not only managed to pluck these plants from a fairly high window sill, but then to strip them completely of their spines and leave the naked cacti standing upright on the floor, looking decidedly embarrassed with their predicament. I can only presume he ate the spines, as they were never seen again. They didn't even appear from the other end as a sad impersonation of a porcupine.

I took off to my library and borrowed all the dog-training manuals they had. Showing remarkable self-control, I managed to stop myself from beating him over the head with them, and read through them thoroughly. Feeling fully clued up, I began my newly learned 'desensitisation programme'. After two weeks of going through the rigmarole of pretending to go out, leaving Hovis for a bit longer each time, trying to familiarise him with being on his own, I'd almost made it to half an hour. The neighbours must have seen me skulking around but obviously just thought I was casing my own joint. Finally, with Hovis acting like a textbook case of impeccability, the big day arrived when I was to go out for real. I followed exactly the same routine that I'd been doing for the last fortnight and left. When I returned – total Bedlam! Obviously he'd not been reading the same books as me.

In my final act of sheer desperation I telephoned our vet. Luckily for me, one of our veterinary nurses specialises in animal behaviour and I went through everything with her – what basic training he'd had, how he was treated in the house, where he slept etc. We came to the conclusion that Hovis thought of himself as more than just a dog. He was living under the misguided illusion that he was either the god of all dogs, or worse than that, human. With the vet nurse's help we managed to convince him that although he was very special, when all was said and done, he was still only a dog. For a time he was, in fact, described in our house, in hushed tones of course, as a dog with 'special needs'.

The first manoeuvre in our bid to change Hovis from Saddam Hussein into Mary Poppins, was to get him to sleep in the kitchen. As described in the chapter SLEEPING, we achieved this much more easily than we ever dared hope. We were also advised to make him go and lie on his bed at various times during the day, even when we were only in the next room. Seemingly small details like this, coupled with dominance techniques like not letting him through doorways before us and occasionally ignoring his demands for attention, all helped to show Hovis that, although he was a valued member of the family, he was not the most important one.

It is for this reason also that dog flaps can, for some dogs, be a very bad idea. With these flaps installed, the dog has complete control over his own comings and goings. He no longer needs you to let him in and out. In fact, if he ever mastered the manual dexterity to use a tin opener, you'd be completely redundant. However, if your dog has to ask to go out, he is constantly being subtly reminded that you are the boss and you have control over when he can go out, and when he is made to come back in. Having said all that, there aren't many dog flaps fitted into Great Dane households. They're usually just called doors.

I have to admit that at the start of Hovis's rehabilitation, I was a bit worried that it would change his character too much and turn him into a big girl's blouse. The only real changes, though, were for the better. To this day, he still occasionally struts his stuff like a cocky beggar, but give him that certain look like you mean business, and his strut instantly turns into 'rubber puppy'. I can honestly say that he is now a delight to live with, and is completely trustworthy when left on his own, but the bitter memories of Hurricane Hovis have not yet been erased from my long-term memory.

You may find that you have a particularly dominant animal and will therefore need to be always on your guard, as if you do have a 'wanna be' dog (or bitch) he may make a bid for the top at any time. Don't ever let him do something once, if you're not prepared to let him do it all the time. It isn't fair and will confuse him. That's not to say that your relationship with him should be spoiled by you watching his every move just in case he should sneeze without asking permission. There is a happy medium, and you'll know, with time, just how much 'give' you can allow your dog.

Sometimes, in a half-hearted and feeble attempt to overthrow me as pack leader, Hovis will stand next to an open doorway looking over his shoulder, waiting for me. Just as I reach the doorway, he will attempt to scuttle through before me. All the time I can tell he's watching to see what I'm going to do about it. On these occasions, because I'm wise to his games, I always call him back and make him wait so I can go through first. In fact, you can see from his expression that he even expects to be called back, but that doesn't stop him from trying again later.

If your dog is in the habit of making the occasional bid for the top, these attempts should become fewer after his first birthday. It will gradually sink in to his mind that you are, and always will be, 'top dog'.

Hovis now sleeps quietly when left on his own, as

he knows he hasn't been permanently abandoned and we will be returning in a short while. If, however, you have a very active dog, I have heard a lot said in favour of the cube-shaped 'balls' in which you put food so your dog can entertain himself rolling it about to try to get it out. We did try this when Hovis was at the height of his destructive phase, stuffing a 'Kong' with some treats. However, as Hovis was not a very food-orientated puppy, coupled with the fact that he has always had an incredibly short attention span, we found it no help. He would give it a cursory sniff, poke it with his nose and, when nothing fell out, he would lie on top of it, totally defeating the object.

It may be no consolation if you're going through this trying phase, but rest assured, it will pass.

THE NOSE TO TAIL TOUR
(Which end to avoid)

Nose
A large, rubbery object whose great purpose seems to be informing your dog where his face stops and the rest of the world starts. It is also the perfect tool for breath sniffing when he thinks you might be secretly eating something without telling him.

Mouth
This huge cavern is used to store a variety of objects for safekeeping. Hovis's collection to date includes:– tea towels, socks, tee shirts, gloves, hats, a selection of children's toys, dead, regurgitated mice, dead, but still warm rabbits. These items are secretly smuggled in, only for him to give the game away later by 'putting his hat on'.

Lips
The most important use of these droopy flaps is to be draped over the above items, thereby concealing them from suspicious humans. With a very lippy Dane, his outward appearance can appear perfectly normal but, on hoisting up these dangling flaps and peering through his teeth, you may find he is hiding something you thought you'd lost days ago.

Hovis likes to run around, head down in long grass (preferably wet or frosty) trailing his flaps through it. I don't know why, but it keeps him happy.

Eyes

There is not much to be said about a dog's eyes that hasn't been said in any number of dog books already. All breeds of dogs have the most beautiful eyes, and all breeds of dogs know exactly how to use them to their best advantage. Hovis can wangle another piece of Red Leicester from me by doing nothing but looking at me in a loving manner.

Ears

These can be very useful as directional aids. If flopped over the head in the style of the 'bald man swoop' – your dog is in a crosswind. If both ears are waving behind him – he's running. If they are pricked and pointed towards you – you have your dog's undivided attention, for once.

I'm grateful that the ridiculous practice of ear cropping is illegal in this country. Personally, I prefer a Great Dane's ears to look natural. Cropping their ears, I believe, makes them look aggressive. This is surely the wrong impression to give of any breed of dog, least of all this one.

Head

I think that the bump, which a Great Dane has at the back of his skull, is a handy peg for nature to hook the loose skin of his head on. This stops his face from completely sliding off when he bends forward.

Neck

This is used to propel the above-mentioned head into various sensitive parts of your body – with force. And, although they aren't there when your dog is a puppy, as he matures he will develop Frankenstein-like seams in his neck (minus the nuts and bolts) when he's a few months old.

Front Legs

If permitted, these will be hoisted off the ground and
hooked around your neck, forcing you to stagger under
the immense weight of the beast. This will have the
effect of making you both look like a very unusual
couple doing a smoochy dance.

Front Paws

To the best of my knowledge, these are the friendly
Dane puppy's only form of self-defence. They are
brought down, sometimes with great force, on top of
anything, from what is perceived to be a vicious
attacker, to an incredibly minor irritation, very effec-
tively pinning the poor unfortunate annoyance to the
floor. It might be better to keep the hamster away
from your dog while he's young and still practising this
trick.

Back

The most outstanding thing about your dog's back is
its length. Because of this, Great Danes find it awkward to turn round – they usually prefer to reverse out
of tight spaces. Sadly, they are not blessed with the
benefit of 'Warning! Dog Reversing' alarms. The back
is also used for lying upside-down on and waving the
legs about, looking ridiculous.

Hind Quarters

Danes are very good in reverse, and will happily back
up to, and park their behind on your sofa, or your lap
if you're already sitting down.

On the downside, this is also the end you need the
poopscoop for. Your Great Dane will produce a lot of
poop. Always, always clean up after your dog. Dogs are
already much maligned; be a responsible owner and
don't give the dog-haters any more ammunition.

Dewclaws

Keep your dog's dewclaws well trimmed, as it's eye-wateringly painful when they are scraped down the back of your leg. This can sometimes happen when your Dane is asking for your attention, or when he's trying to trip you up as you're running away from him.

Although the dewclaws can damage your furniture, trousers, tights and skin, I still don't feel that this is a good enough reason for removing them routinely from every single puppy born. A better reason is that he might catch them in something and badly damage himself.

Tail

Great Danes don't so much wag their tails, as wave them about. Sometimes this will be done in a slow, gentle manner. At other times the tail will be waving frantically. It will knock your ornaments off, it will send the cat flying and it will have your eye out, just because your dog is pleased to see you.

On a more serious note – though it is not common, if your Dane does manage to damage his tail, it can be very hard to repair. This is because the tail is an awkward shape to keep a bandage on, and you can't really stop him wagging it.

Thankfully, Great Danes aren't docked. I often wonder what the pro-dockers' argument would be on the subject of Danes, as the one usually trotted out by them with regards to Boxers, Dobermans etc., is that they are docked for their own safety! They argue that the tails must be cut off, because, if left in the natural state, they are thin and whip-like, and would be continually damaged from getting bashed on objects. Well I'm sorry, but the Great Dane also has a fairly thin, whip-like tail, which has never, ever been routinely docked, and they don't seem to damage them that often.

I get very annoyed at the normally rational people who can't see anything wrong with cutting bits off their dogs in the name of tradition. When a surgeon approaches them wielding his scalpel and uttering the words, "Don't worry, you don't need it," perhaps they may view their own actions toward their dogs differently.

Overall Appearance
The overall appearance of the Great Dane as an adult will resemble that of a thoroughbred racehorse. He should be capable of the most beautiful, almost dressage-like paces. To watch a Dane showing off these paces is pure magic. He should be lean, yet muscular. He will look as if he's fully aware that everyone is looking at him. He will stand proud and almost pose for them. He will strut his stuff along with the best of them. He will look truly magnificent.

DANE-ISH HABITS
(Entertaining the troops)

A s I have only ever owned one Great Dane, this chapter is compiled from watching my own dog, watching various friends' Danes, discussing all things 'Dane-ish' with people in the know, and through reading any Great Dane literature I could get my hands on.

These traits may be common in other breeds, but I haven't studied any of the other breeds, so therefore have no knowledge of their particular habits. I do know, however, as a previous cat owner, that Great Danes aren't at all like cats.

Body Rubbing
This activity starts when very young. As a small puppy, Hovis would always, before going to sleep, scoot himself along the bottom of the sofa. This action was very similar to a cat rubbing itself along your leg, only much faster and with much more urgency. As he grew up, his body rubbing progressed to hedges and trees, and then on to practically anything which would withstand the full weight. He does still do this, but there aren't many objects left standing which can tolerate this treatment without collapsing under the strain.

Fly-Bys
The fly-by will be done in the field or the garden if he can build up enough speed. He will be in a flat-out

gallop, get you in his sights and 'lock on'. He will already have judged perfectly the distance between you and him, so as he reaches you, he can skim the side of your body with his.

Sometimes, when he's in an exceptionally good mood, he will, if coming at you from behind, at the moment of impact, leap into the air, so, as you look over your shoulder, he'll whiz by at eye level.

Bouncing

All this takes is a hedge or fence, and an insatiable urge to know what is on the other side.

If the fence is only a little bit taller than your dog, he will make do by visibly straightening his legs and neck, and standing on tiptoes. However, if he's running loose and the fence is quite a bit taller than he is, he will start bouncing. His back feet will remain on the ground while the rest of him is launched skywards. From this position he will be able to peer over a six-foot fence with ease. On landing, he will run a little way, then re-launch himself ready for another look. If he's well balanced, he can hold his 'airborne' position for a few seconds and make himself look like a much overgrown meerkat.

If you happen to be on the other side of the fence and therefore on the receiving end of this ambush, be prepared. Remember his face and ears will still be going upwards for a few seconds after the rest of him has stopped. Gravity will have the effect of making his face appear to grin at you like the Joker from *Batman*.

Headresting

In your Great Dane's opinion, one of the reasons you exist is so that when he's feeling a little weary he can rest his head on you. When you're relaxing watching TV, not only will he stand about two inches in front of you so you can kindly scratch his chest or inside his leg, but you will be expected to bear the full weight of his enormous head on your shoulder at the same time. It will appear to increase in weight as the minutes pass until it will feel as if you're sinking under the Rock of Gibraltar.

You will be expected to carry out this duty whenever and wherever he chooses – perhaps when he's on the back seat of the car and he's decided that his head is too heavy for him to manage on his own. You may even be unlucky enough to have a dog like Hovis who, after a particularly energetic time bouncing around the field looking over hedges, realises that his head is too much trouble to carry back home all by himself and will hook it through your arm so you can support it for him. So far I haven't had to explain to people that I'm not actually pulling him along by the head, but I've a feeling it won't be long.

Grunting

While he is a puppy, this noise manages to emerge as a cute, gentle squeak, but as your dog matures, it will develop into a full-blown 'old man groan'. It is usually reserved for the exact leg-buckling moment when your dog is arranging himself for sleep. As his body is sinking to the floor, it will expel air (through the mouth) with a long drawn out groan, almost as if your dog is deflating. Not being an old man, or a Great Dane, I can only guess that this noise is made to signify extreme pleasure.

Gift Giving

If you leave your dog on his own, when you return he will feel compelled to run off and find something to give to you. Hovis gets so single-minded in his compulsion, that I now leave him a hide bone for this purpose. It gives him something to chew while I'm out, and on my return he doesn't have to get into a frenzy finding something to give me. He will pick his bone up and 'put his hat on' while strutting backwards and forwards waiting for me to take it from him.

Stealing

To be completely fair, Hovis doesn't steal things in a malicious way. When he's taken the selected item, usually a tea towel, he'll come and own up by 'putting his hat on'. If the washing machine door has been left open, he'll occasionally help himself to a sock. But again, he'll come and tell on himself straight away. If anything, this little hobby of his teaches me to be tidy and not leave anything lying around.

Headstands

This activity is carried out when Hovis is in one of his particularly stupid moods. First, he'll run around in a frenzy looking for somewhere to perform this action. When a suitable place, usually an armchair, has been found, he will tuck his head in close to his chest and scrub the top of it on the seat of the chair in a grinding motion.

If he can't get to an armchair before the urge takes him over completely, then he'll do it on his bed. As his bed is at floor level, this usually results in him doing a headstand. If he is travelling at speed by the time he reaches his bed, he will perform a spectacular somersault. Although this can't possibly do him any good, it doesn't seem to deter him. He occasionally likes to do these somersaults while walking in the field.

Collapsing

Your dog will probably perfect this manoeuvre while quite young. He aims his body towards the place he's decided to sleep, and just as he arrives he will drop like a stone. Not for him the strange circling dance of the older dog (although that will come later); he will just hit the ground as if he's been shot. Once down, he might make a token gesture at arranging himself into a more composed heap, but usually not.

Parking
A Great Dane likes to 'park' himself on things. This usually involves first eyeing up the object. It could be your armchair or sofa; it doesn't matter whether you're already sitting in it, as your lap will be even better. He will then position himself in front of his chosen resting-place, with his back legs just touching it. From this angle, he can look over his shoulder for a little fine-tuning before shifting into reverse and plonking himself down. If it happens to be on your lap, pleading with him to get off will have no effect whatsoever, and trying to push him away will only result in him leaning backwards and cutting off your oxygen supply. Try asking someone to go into the kitchen and shout "Dinner-time!" If he's already eaten, you're in serious trouble. Remember that your frail old Aunt Mabel probably won't appreciate your dog lap-dancing all over her.

Leaning
The degree of laziness built in to a Great Dane's genes can be measured by the fact that he can't even be bothered to support his own body weight for more than about forty-six seconds. After this he will align himself up against your legs and make himself as comfortable as is possible while remaining vertical. He won't do this to other people though; this practice is strictly reserved for you, the chosen one. His favourite time to do this will be when you've stopped in the street to talk to somebody. He is useful as a leg warmer in the winter.

Pawing

This is something *every* Great Dane does. In fact I have
never seen a Dane NOT do this. It is a variation on the
usual 'give me a paw' trick which people perform with
their dogs. With your Dane, however, you won't need to
ask him to do this, he will just lift his front leg up
and offer it to you. This can be triggered by a variety
of reasons, from feeling a bit lonely and asking for your
company, to being bored while you talk to someone out
on a walk. It is a very appealing and endearing trait,
which will serve to reinforce your bond with your dog.

Barking Backwards

Although Hovis could not be called a coward as such,
he is a little bit of a girl's blouse when it comes to either
new things, or new situations. Not for him the stride-
right-in, gung-ho attitude of the bolder dog. He prefers
to take his time. He will stand back from possible
danger, and from this safety zone will tentatively stretch
his nose forward to investigate. If he's not convinced
of his personal safety, he will go quickly into reverse
while making a sound somewhere between a cough and
a bark. He will continue to make this 'hrumphffing'
sound until he has either scared off the potential threat,
or mustered enough bottle to take a closer look.

Slobbering

You must be aware that *all* Great Danes slobber.
Admittedly, they aren't in the super league: I believe
that is reserved for the Saint Bernards, Newfoundlands
and Mastiffs. However, in the slobber Olympics, they
would get the Silver every time. You can try to minimise
your chance of having to spend every Sunday morning
washing down your walls by choosing your puppy from
less 'lippy' parents although, due to the shape of a
Dane's face, even that doesn't necessarily mean that

you'll escape altogether. And even among the lippy Danes, some have naturally drier mouths than others, and you won't encounter the slobber problem with those dogs as much. Unfortunately for you, eight-week-old puppies don't have labels on them telling you which is which.

Should you find yourself the owner of a serious slobberer, I found the easiest way of dealing with it is to wipe it up with a dry cloth first, before a final rinse with soapy water. Any attempt at wiping it with the soapy water first will just result in you smearing it about a bit.

GENERAL CARE
(Smartening up his act)

This chapter is simply a guide to general day to day maintenance. With regard to your dog's health, I can only say, use your intuition and if it ever worries you, take him straight to the vet. I know vets can be expensive, but how much is your dog worth to you? Have a look at getting him insured. It really isn't too expensive, you can choose what level of cover you want, and it could save you from a frighteningly hideous bill at some stage in your dog's life. A word of warning though: check the small print, as a few companies charge extra for the 'giants'.

Everything I've ever read or been told about the Great Dane breed, says that they require hardly any grooming. I must obviously own the only Dane in the world which moults every time the central heating kicks in. My vet tells me that, in this sybaritic age, dogs and cats have lost the need for the twice-yearly moult of the olden days, and now simply lose hair all year round. I have found that if I don't give Hovis a quick brush over at least every other day, not only does his hair drop out like Christmas tree needles, but he also develops that 'dusty dog' look that dogs kept in kennels always seem to have. I use a rubber brush, a little like a horse's rubber curry-comb, and have found nothing better for getting the dead hairs out of his coat. Then a quick going over with a normal bristle brush over his body and head puts a shine on him, and that really is all it takes.

It is possible to buy a variety of coat care chemicals for your dog. From a huge array of shampoos and spray-on coat-shine, to stuff which stops your dog smelling like a dog (just what did you expect him to smell of?), the list could go on forever. Don't waste your money; you really don't need any of these things. A good coat comes from inside. If you're feeding him a good quality food, this will show in his general appearance. Like-wise, if his diet is lacking, so too will be his appearance. My dog usually only has a couple of baths a year, unless of course he has rolled in something which necessitates a speedy clean-up operation.

You could give your dog's face a daily wipe with a damp cloth. There's no telling whether dogs like a wash in the mornings, but I like to think that it leaves them feeling a bit more refreshed.

While giving your dog a brush over, keep an eye out for any lumps, bumps or scratches, which may need attention. Great Danes sometimes get the odd bump appearing under the skin. Hovis gets these and they don't bother him in the slightest. They usually disappear after a couple of days without any treatment, only to pop up again in a different location later in the month.

Take a look in your dog's ears. Dogs with floppy ears sometimes suffer from an excessive build-up of muck. Apparently, in the wild, where all animals have either erect or open ears (there is no such thing as a wild animal with floppy ears), they don't suffer from ear problems very much. This is either due to the air circulating through the ear canal, or it's just that no one's ever looked down a tiger's ear and lived to tell us what was in there. If your dog's ears look a bit dirty, give them a wipe. You can buy special ear wipes for this, or just use baby wet wipes. If they seem really dirty, or he's scratching them, or shaking his head a lot, take him to the vet, as he might have ear mites. These are a common gift given, with joy, from cats to dogs. The vet will give you some drops to put in, but you must treat the cat as well. That's presuming the cat belongs to you. There's no need to go prowling the neighbour-hood armed with a bottle of eardops, searching out all the local moggies, unless of course you want to.

If you're really dedicated, you could go the whole hog and brush your dog's teeth. I know it's extremely bene-ficial to them, and I should do it, but I'm ashamed to say I don't. I do give Hovis a product called 'Breatheze'. These large green dog sweets claim to clean his teeth and freshen his breath. At the time of writing, his teeth appear to be healthy and tartar free. Feeding dry dog food is beneficial to the teeth too, as it acts as a mild abrasive.

Keep an eye on your dog's claws. If you don't exercise him on hard ground very much, you'll need to trim them. Get your vet to show you how to do this properly as, even if your dog does get a lot of roadwork, you'll need to keep his dewclaws down. If you've never done them before, you'll need to be shown how far to cut them because, if you cut them too short, you'll cut into the quick, and they'll bleed a lot.

Although it might not seem to come under the category of general care, while you're attending to these matters you will be getting your dog to sit, lie down, give you his paws etc., and by doing this you will be reinforcing your authority over him and reminding him (and yourself) that you are the boss. Don't put up with him squirming and wriggling to get away from you. He needs to accept that you can, and will, do these things to him whenever you feel like it.

Although Great Danes are quite low-maintenance dogs, I have been in the unfortunate position of having to bath Hovis due to his rolling in something vile, on a

couple of occasions up to date. Luckily, on both occasions the weather was quite warm, which meant that I
could wash Hovis outside. I washed all of him except
his head, which I left until last as I'd read that, when
washing your dog, if you leave the head until last he
won't shake himself. But he did.

If you find yourself having to wash your Great Dane,
try to dry him as quickly as possible. Whenever I
washed Hovis, although I did him outside when the
weather was hot, he got an attack of the shivers. As
soon as you've finished rinsing your dog and he's
shaken himself, take him inside (where he will promptly shake himself again all over your furniture), towel
him off, then get him warm and dry by whatever means
you have. Try not to laugh at your dog when he's wet:
you might give him a complex. The problem is that
when Great Danes are wet, the fur on their head goes
all woolly and they look like bears. If you can't stifle
your mirth, and your dog does catch you laughing at
him, he will look down his nose with the utter contempt
that only a Dane can so well express.

More and more people are, quite rightly, taking
advantage of the ease and accessibility of the permanent methods of identification for their dogs. Apart
from the name-tag on his collar, which he must have
by law, you can have your dog either tattooed or
microchipped. A number is tattooed into his ear, or
inside his back leg. This number, unique to your dog,
is kept on a register and, if he is picked up, you will be
traced and informed.

Similarly, a tiny microchip can be inserted under
your dog's skin, usually in the scruff of his neck. This
microchip also has a unique number. When your dog
is found, most canine organisations including council
dog wardens, animal shelters etc., have a scanner,
which reads the microchip and shows your number.

Again, you can be traced through a register. Sadly, the microchip does not work like a 'Trakback' does on a car: there is no TV monitor with lots of little blips whizzing around on it like Space Invaders, as all the microchipped dogs go out for their walks. Don't forget, if you move house, to inform the company of your dog's change of address. You don't want him delivered back to your old house should he go missing.

Obviously, whichever method of identification you choose for your dog, you are still required by law to have a collar with some kind of ID on it. Although the disc on Hovis's collar carries my name, address and telephone number, it doesn't have his name on it. This is because, if someone did want to take him away, he would be more likely to follow him or her if they were using his name. Or carrying a piece of cheese. Or even if they just looked nice.

As general maintenance goes, the Great Dane doesn't really require any special treatment. The treatment you would give to any other short-coated breed of dog is all he needs. Just much more of it.

HELPING THE AGED
(One and over)

By about the age of one, your dog will probably just be starting to go grey around the muzzle. I say probably as I did once come across a Dane bitch whose owner swore her dog was five years old and there wasn't a grey hair in sight. Although this dusting of grey will have the delightful effect of making your dog look like a distinguished country gent, it is still a bit of a shame, as all the rest of him will still be in its prime.

Life with your Dane should by now be mostly nothing but pleasure. You will both have survived the trials and tribulations of puppyhood and the sometimes exasperating 'teenage' months. By now your dog should both know, and be happy with, his place in your pack (never let him presume this is anywhere but at the bottom). Although still extremely capable and often willing to remind you that he is still a young dog, he will also happily potter around your home without knocking stuff over all the time.

If you have other animals, they will by now have forged a loving, permanent bond with your dog – or packed their bags and left home. Sometimes animals just have a funny way of showing their affection. My cats, if they could talk, would all swear blind that they hate not only the very ground that Hovis walks on, but the air he breathes as well. However, if they think nobody is watching, they show obvious cat-like signs of affection such as not sticking their claws into his face at the slightest opportunity, and not taking up all his bed, but leaving him a generous 10cm corner piece to lie on. Perhaps, because he was brought up with five cats, Hovis has developed certain cat-like mannerisms. He will rub his face and body against your leg like a cat, although not quite with the same self-centred 'pervert on a train' urgency that cats do.

Your dog will, if he's had the correct training, be very amenable to your tending to his grooming, claw clipping etc. and, if he's been blessed with an extremely sociable character, even worming. I've found that when most Great Danes see you coming with the flea spray, they'll put up a token gesture of pretending to run away, but quickly seem to realise that resistance is futile and give in relatively gracefully. Danes have a particular body language, which they reserve for these occasions. It is a sort of dignified acceptance seen at these times, and also at dog shows.

Go to any dog show and you'll notice that most of the other breeds will be excited, barking and some of them even on the point of uncontrollable hysteria. Take a walk down the Great Dane end and it all goes quiet. Although the Danes will probably be having just as much fun as the other breeds, they seem so laid back about it all. Not for them the frantic tail wagging, the jumping up to greet everyone, the getting caught up in the hustle and bustle of the atmosphere. They enjoy it in their own way. They take everything in their stride. When woken up (no mean feat) and asked to leave his bench, the Dane seems able, on entering the judging area, to switch on his charm, poise and charisma for the judge, only to revert back to his subconscious, semi-comatose state on leaving the ring.

An odd trend I've come across with older Danes is their tendency to run away when let off the lead. I'm not sure if this is down to bad training, or if it is actually a breed trait. Thankfully, we don't have this trouble with Hovis. I'm not claiming any glory for him being exceptionally well trained. He's not. We have success-fully managed to train him to stay near us without realising that we were doing it. All we used to do was to walk off in another direction every time it looked as if Hovis had anticipated where we would be going. He would go bounding off in front of us; convinced he knew our direction. On glancing over his shoulder, he would see that we had, in fact, gone off another way. This would take him by surprise and he would very quickly return to us, thinking he would be left behind. If, on the odd occasion, he was too engrossed in what he was doing to notice, we would hide behind a tree or bush. Then, when he did finally turn around, he would not be able to see us anywhere. This would have the effect of making him rush straight back to sniff us out. Surprisingly, we have not ended up with a totally psychotic dog with a huge inferiority complex, but one which, although running loose, will keep glancing over his shoulder just to keep an eye on us.

I did read in a dog training manual that a foolproof way of getting your dog to come back to you is to lie flat out, spread-eagled on the ground. I've not managed to find out if the person who wrote this actually lives in Britain and is therefore aware that you could only practise this method for about two weeks out of the year. The other fifty would result in you becoming so wet and muddy that you would be completely camou-flaged, and even if your dog was equipped with a pair of binoculars and a compass, he still wouldn't be able to find you. I have to admit that I have never seen any-body try this method out, so cannot vouch for whether it works or not. What I do know is that I can think of a million other places I'd rather be than lying flat on the ground in front of a Great Dane travelling at speed and heading my way.

Your older Dane is a great friend to have in your home. He is happy as long as he is with you. If you watch Dane owners, you'll see that they all are very, very close to their dogs and treat them very much as part of the family. Because Danes are large dogs, they are always 'in your space' and at hip level. Therefore you don't need to bend down to stroke them, which means you find yourself touching them perhaps more than you would a smaller dog. If allowed, Hovis will follow me around the house, sometimes just sleeping outside my office door.

In summing up my life with a Great Dane so far, I have found the breed to be very loyal and trusting. They don't respond to strangers instantly, but once they have taken a fancy to certain 'outsiders', they will be friends for life. Hovis is a little wary too, of other dogs, and gets jealous if I should stroke one. This may stem from the fact that he has been an 'only dog', who hasn't learned to 'share his toys' yet. I've watched breeders with many Danes, and they don't seem to have a problem with their packs. As soon as there's stroking being given out, each dog will take his place in the queue and wait patiently until it's his turn, diplomatically moving out of the way afterwards for the next in line.

Hovis gets on well with the cats I have but, again, he does tend to become jealous if I pay them any attention. However, because I am aware of the potential trouble this could cause if ignored, I make him wait while the cats get stroked, and they are also fed before him. All these actions remind him of his place in the 'family pack'.

FINAL WORDS
(Nothing like a Dane)

You may have gathered by now that I am completely besotted with the Great Dane. If you already have your Dane, I won't need to explain why, you'll already know. If you're still just running through the idea of getting one, I'm not sure I can explain why. Everybody who owns a Dane will tell you the same thing: there is just something about them. You won't ever get an answer to what that 'something' is. We're not being secretive, we just don't know what it is ourselves. Another thing you'll hear many times is that once you've owned a Great Dane, you'll never go back to another breed.

I have owned other dogs in the past; some cross breeds, some pedigrees, so it's not as if I am simply smitten with that unconditional love which most dogs will give you. It is much, much more than this. For complete and utter devotion to his family, for a gentle, dignified, loyal friend, there really is nothing like a Dane.

There are some special responsibilities involved in owning a Dane and I will list some of them for you. By comparison with small dogs, they can be expensive to feed, especially when they are puppies, as it is of paramount importance that they have the best food while their bones are developing. They also need more worming medication, as this is calculated by the weight of the dog. This is not nit-picking, since you will end up with a dog weighing at least 120lbs or more, requiring large quantities of everything and any trip to the vet is usually expensive. Any collars, leads, bowls or toys you buy for your Dane will have to be 'Supa Doopa' sized versions. And Supa Doopa sizes generally mean Supa Doopa prices.

Dane-owning may need a change of lifestyle to suit your dog. Think of the size of his bed. Where will it go? Can you train yourself to be extra tidy and not leave things out on the worktops or tables etc? A Great Dane can, and will, help himself to anything you've left on your worktops. To him, this isn't stealing, he just presumes you've forgotten to give it to him. Do you have the time and inclination for all the extra housework caused by enormous muddy feet and a layer of dog hair?

A Great Dane doesn't just fit discreetly and quietly into your house. He is always very obvious. You can't step over him, he blocks doorways, and he knocks things over. And, although he can quite happily manage if you only have a postage-stamp-sized garden, he would, if given the choice, prefer one large enough for him to patrol and stretch his legs in.

What will you do with him when you visit people who don't like dogs, or just can't accommodate him in their house? This last question is especially important and worth giving a great deal of thought, as your Dane will desperately want to go everywhere with you. Can you enjoy a holiday knowing he's in kennels? On the few occasions we had no other choice than to leave Hovis in kennels, he didn't like them at all and refused to eat while there. This isn't unusual with Danes. As a breed, they so much want to be part of the family that they dislike being separated from you for even a day, and this can manifest itself in starving themselves. A breeder local to us told us, "What a Dane loses in three days, it'll take three months to put back on." Because of this, we now only ever leave Hovis in kennels as a 'day case', dropping him off in the morning and collecting him in the evening. Some people wouldn't be prepared to let their dog's needs rule their life like this. We are. Are you?

I don't mean to put you off getting a Great Dane, but better to consider these things before buying your dog, rather than afterwards when it's far too late. Your local RSPCA or dog rescue centre could probably tell you of people who thought that getting a Great Dane seemed like a good idea at the time. They will also tell you how particularly hard it is to re-home not just Great Danes, but any of the giant breeds. Please, please don't buy a Great Dane without a great deal of thought beforehand. Apart from the absolute misery you might cause the dog, their purchase price remains in the higher range (anything from £500 to £800), and you would be throwing an awful lot of money away if you found you had to give him up.

If you haven't been put off, and are still convinced a Great Dane is for you, let me assure you, for all the extra amount of work your dog will cause, he will give you double that back in his love for you. He will warn away strangers with his baritone bark, he will be the cause of conversation with other dog walkers, he will be an excellent, if heavy, foot warmer when you're watching TV, but most importantly, he will ALWAYS be there for you. He will lay his life down for you if need be.

If you're the owner of a young Dane puppy, you're probably looking at him now with his rubber legs, huge knees and his ears flopped across his head, with that confused look on his baggy face, thinking that perhaps yours is different, perhaps you got a 'wrong-un', perhaps he won't turn out right: but he will. In just a few short months your gangling, wrinkle headed, possibly frustrating little puppy will metamorphose into a handsome, magnificent, proud dog.

ADDRESS OF NATIONAL GREAT DANE RESCUE

Mrs. Val Harverson
Brook Farm
Sellindge
Ashford
Kent
TN25 6HL

Tel: 01303 814959